Intervention on Trial

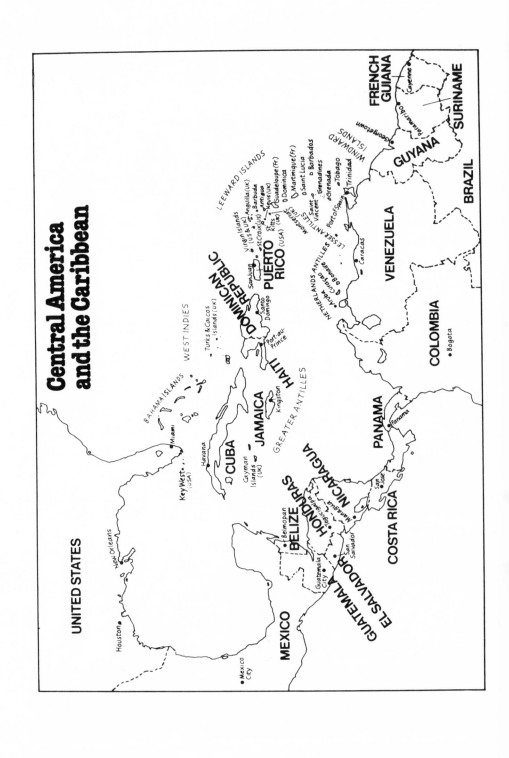

Central America and the Caribbean

Intervention on Trial

The New York War Crimes
Tribunal on Central America
and the Caribbean

Edited by
Paul Ramshaw and Tom Steers

With the Assistance
of
Kevin Krajick

A Project of the National Lawyers Guild
New York City Chapter
Central America Task Force

New York
Westport, Connecticut
London

Grateful acknowledgment is made for permission to reprint the maps and photographs that appear on the following pages of this book:

On page ii, from Pearce, Jenny, *Under the Eagle* (London, UK: Latin America Bureau, Research and Action, Ltd., 1981), p. viii. Reprinted with permission. On pages 2, 52, 64, and 72 from Stanford Central America Action Network, *Revolution in Central America* (Boulder, CO: Westview Press, 1983), pp. xvi, xvii, xviii, and xix. Reprinted with permission. On page 114, Brizan, George, *Grenada: Island of Conflict* (London, UK: Zed Books, Ltd., 1984), p. xi. Reprinted with permission. On page 130, copyright © 1960 by Leo Huberman and Paul M. Sweezy. Reprinted by permission of Monthly Review Foundation. On pages 44, 47, and 48, reprinted with permission of Paolo Bosio. On pages 43, 45, 46, 47, 48, and 49, reprinted with permission of Comision de Derechos Humanos de El Salvador.

Library of Congress Cataloging-in-Publication Data

New York War Crimes Tribunal on Central America
   and the Caribbean (1984 : New York, N.Y.)
   Intervention on trial.

   "A project of the National Lawyers Guild,
New York City Chapter."
   1. Central America — Politics and government —
1979–   2. Atrocities — Central America —
History — 20th century. 3. Intervention (Inter-
national law) 4. United States — Foreign relations —
Central America. 5. Central America — Foreign
relations — United States. 6. United States —
Foreign relations — 1945–   . I. Ramshaw, Paul.
II. Steers, Tom. III. Krajick, Kevin. IV. National
Lawyers Guild. New York City Chapter. V. Title.

F1439.5.N49 1984   972.8'05   86-30342
ISBN 0-275-92188-3 (alk. paper)
ISBN 0-275-92189-1 (pbk. : alk. paper)

Library of Congress Catalog Card Number: 86-30342
ISBN: 0-275-92188-3 cloth
        0-275-92189-1 paperback

First published in 1987

Praeger Publishers, 521 Fifth Avenue, New York, NY 10175
A division of Greenwood Press, Inc.

Printed in the United States of America

The paper used in this book complies with the Permanent Paper Standard issued by the National Information Standards Organization (Z39.48-1984).

10 9 8 7 6 5 4 3 2 1

It is not in dispute, among rational people with some concern for the facts, that the United States' command is responsible for major crimes, in the layman's sense of the term. What we may reasonably ask is whether the acts that are documented beyond dispute are also crimes in the lawyer's sense — recognizing that when we raise this question, it is not the war that is on trial, but the law. We are asking — if we are serious — whether the law is a sufficiently precise and delicate instrument so that it can label a monstrous crime as a violation of the law.

> Noam Chomsky
> *For Reasons of State*
> (1973)

If our government wages war in our name, we must assume the profound responsibility to wage peace and seek justice.

> National Lawyers Guild
> Central America Task
> Force (1984)

The National Lawyers Guild is an association dedicated to the need for basic change in the structure of our political and economic system. We seek to unite the lawyers, law students, legal workers, and jailhouse lawyers of America in an organization which shall function as an effective political and social force in the service of the people, to the end that human rights shall be regarded as more sacred than property interests. Our aim is to bring together all those who regard adjustments to new conditions as more important than veneration of precedent; who recognize the importance of safeguarding and extending the rights of workers, women, farmers, and minority groups upon whom the welfare of the entire nation depends; who seek actively to eliminate racism; who work to maintain and protect our civil rights and civil liberties in the face of persistent attacks upon them; and who look upon the law as an instrument for the protection of the people, rather than for their repression.

Preamble to the National
Lawyers Guild
Constitution

Contents

Foreword

After working for one year as a physician in a rural area of El Salvador, I returned to the United States in March 1983 anxious to make known what I had experienced. I, like most U.S. citizens, was under the impression that hearings conducted by Congress are forums in which the principal objective is a search for truth. The House Subcommittee on Human Rights and International Organizations was holding hearings on whether El Salvador had met certain human rights conditions, before Congress could allocate supplemental military aid to El Salvador. I traveled to Washington, D.C., and was informed that it would be necessary to be interviewed and approved by the committee staff before I could testify. I explained the terms of my service in El Salvador: As a Quaker, I wouldn't bear arms; I expected to work with civilians; my medical neutrality would be respected. Specifically, I could treat anyone without regard to political considerations. There were ten thousand civilians under my care, 40 percent of whom were under twelve years of age. I also explained that in accordance with the Geneva Conventions, on occasion, I treated wounded government soldiers and guerrillas. In the previous six months the villages in which I worked had been indiscriminately bombed, rocketed, or strafed on a daily basis with U.S.-supplied aircraft. As a Distinguished Graduate of the U.S. Air Force Academy and a Vietnam veteran, who once flew some of the same planes that were attacking my patients, I was capable of making such observations. Without further questions, the interview was terminated. I was notified that I would not be permitted to testify because I was a "biased witness who would polarize the hearings"! I was eventually permitted to testify, albeit for three minutes, through some parliamentary maneuvering of Ed Feighan (D-Ohio).

The response to my testimony was disbelief. Guazapa, the area that I was describing, was not in some remote jungle. It was only twenty miles from the capital, San Salvador. On a clear day I could see the hotel where the press corps stayed, and yet in that year I saw no U.S. reporters. There had yet to be any U.S. media reports of white phosphorus or napalm use against civilians.

After those hearings several congressmen traveled to El Salvador to question the commander of the air force, Colonel Rafael Bustillo, about my allegations. He responded, "Of course, it is a free-fire zone" — meaning that any of the ten thousand civilians, thirty-two schools, sixteen clinics, or two hospitals were considered legitimate targets. Since that time hundreds, perhaps thousands, of civilians have died and tens of thousands have fled as a result of an aerial war that remains largely unreported.

I don't fault the media entirely. During the first week I was in El

Salvador, four Dutch television journalists were murdered en route to a rural area of the country. Their mutilated bodies were displayed naked in the morgue for the press corps as an objective lesson. A death list of journalists was coincidentally published that day. A dozen journalists have died trying to cover the war in El Salvador.

In 1985 I returned to El Salvador with a congressional delegation. By that time embarrassing reports of indiscrimate bombings had led President Duarte to institute strict guidelines that would prevent civilian casualties. While our delegation was in the capital, an A-37 fighter bomber attacked a government-controlled town just outside of San Salvador. Reporters jumped in their rented cars and rushed to the scene only to be stopped at government roadblocks. Nervous young soldiers said they knew the press had lost the war for the U.S. citizens in Vietnam, and their commander said they wouldn't let it happen in El Salvador. Later that day a U.S. church-sponsored relief worker squatted in the back of a crowded bus and reached the village. She found that a woman and her three children had been killed in an incident that clearly violated all of Duarte's so-called "rules of engagement." When I inquired, the U.S.-embassy human-rights officer said she had investigated the charges and dismissed the incident as "typical guerrilla propaganda." The Salvadoran Air Force denies that the incident ever occurred.

The aerial war has escalated since I left El Salvador. Now U.S.-piloted AC-130 aircraft fly over the countryside at night. Their infrared cameras, capable of sensing the heat of an infant from 10,000 feet, provide targeting information to the Salvadoran Air Force — in direct violation of the War Powers Act. AC-47 gunships, whose multiple machine guns fire .50 calibre bullets, which pierce tree trunks as if they were toothpicks, have rendered useless the covered trenches in which my patients used to take cover. U.S. military aid has provided Hughes 500 helicopters with night vision scopes and electronic Gatling guns capable of placing a bullet in every square foot of a football field every sixty seconds. As a result, civilians can no longer flee these "search and destroy" operations under cover of darkness.

According to U.S. military advisers, the area known as Guazapa is finally "pacified." However, the only peace it knows is the peace of the dead — its ten thousand inhabitants dead, "disappeared," or in refugee camps. If any of them were so fortunate as to flee as far as the United States, they would be deported by Immigration and Naturalization Service agents who claim that "they don't have a legitimate basis to fear persecution."

U.S. citizens whose tax dollars are financing this aerial war largely remain ignorant of it. The situation in El Salvador is just one part of an ever-widening tragedy in Central America to which U.S. policy is contributing. THUS THE INCREDIBLE IMPORTANCE OF THE WAR CRIMES TRIBUNAL ON CENTRAL AMERICA AND THE CARIBBEAN.

Without even realizing it, we as citizens are consenting to policies that violate the moral principles by which we wish to live. Consequently, our integrity as moral beings and the integrity of the political community for which we sacrifice these precepts is undermined. The more morally dubious a foreign adventure, the more certain it is to be wrapped in lies. It was a tribute to the U.S. people that five presidents had to lie to them about the war in Vietnam. It was not a virtue that it took the U.S. people so long to realize it.

We now have the documents that expose the policy that led us into war in Southeast Asia. Authored by George Kennan, top secret State Department document PPS 23 stated unequivocally that "we should cease to talk about vague and — for the Far East — unreal objectives such as human rights, the raising of living standards, and democratization . . . the less we are hampered by idealistic slogans, the better."

What is as disturbing as the current lies themselves is the equanimity with which their exposure is received today when they are justified "in the name of democracy." U.S. policy, as this tribunal so poignantly and tragically demonstrates, has as little to do with democracy in Central America today as it did in Vietnam when PPS 23 was authored.

The record of the Reagan administration speaks for itself "in the name of democracy." Six months ago they sought millions of dollars for a resumption of aid to Jean Claude Duvalier "in the name of democracy." A year ago they sought a hundred million dollars of additional military aid for Ferdinand Marcos "in the name of democracy." Two years ago they sought millions of dollars for a resumption of military aid "in the name of democracy" for the generals in Guatemala, referred to recently as the most incompetent, corrupt, and brutal in that nation's history. And it was only four years ago that once again "in the name of democracy" the administration pressed for a resumption of military aid to the Argentinian junta — the same generals who have recently been convicted of murdering over nine thousand civilians "in the name of democracy."

The resources of the earth and the ingenuity of humanity can provide abundance for all — as long as we are prepared to recognize the diversity of humankind and the variety of ways in which people will seek national fulfillment. This is the U.S. vision of the world — diversity of states, each developing according to its own traditions and its own genius, each solving its own economic and political problems in its own manner, and all bound together by a respect for the rights of others, by a loyalty to the world community, and a faith in the dignity of humankind. This is the American dream on which our own nation was founded. When will we stop denying to others that which we find so precious for ourselves?

This tribunal shows the moral morass into which we are being plunged when the president of the United States calls murderers, rapists, and torturers "the moral equivalent of our founding fathers." When the United States sacrifices its own historic principles of democracy, self-determination, respect for law, and support for international institutions in favor of mindless anticommunism, we jeopardize any claim to moral and political leadership.

Last fall in Great Britain a member of Parliament reminded me that when Iran refused jurisdiction of the World Court in 1979, our State Department said it left them "outside the community of civilized nations." At that time the case against the United States' illegal mining of Nicaraguan ports was being heard in the World Court. Referring to the U.S. refusal to participate in the proceedings, he then asked, "Is the United States today outside the community of civilized nations?" After reading the proceedings of the War Crimes Tribunal on Central America and the Caribbean, I hope you will encourage someone to read them who knows nothing about Central America and then ask that same question, "Are we the United States outside the community of civilized nations today?"

Charles Clements, M.D.
Washington, D.C.
April 1986

Acknowledgments

The War Crimes Tribunal on Central America and the Caribbean brought together many individuals and organizations dedicated to educating the U.S. public about the illegality of U.S. intervention in Central America and the Caribbean. It would be impossible to thank individually all those who spent long hours conceptualizing, organizing, and carrying out the tribunal, of which this book is a record.

Special thanks must be given to the witnesses, many of whom traveled great distances, to present informative and moving testimony that inspired many of those in attendance; the judges, who spent hours listening to testimony and deliberating; the committee, which took on this book as a project: Paul Becker, who stenographically reported the entire proceedings and worked on the production of the book along with Marti Copleman, Cathy Potler, Michael Schneider, Diane Steelman, and other members of the Central America Task Force of the New York City chapter of the National Lawyers Guild, and especially Sofia Sequenzia, whose dedication, energy, and long hours of work made this book a reality; our literary agent, Frances Goldin, for her encouragement and perseverance; and the foundations and individuals whose generous contributions enabled the tribunal to be created.

Introduction

Throughout the twentieth century nations and groups of individuals have conducted tribunals to examine the actions of those accused of war crimes, crimes against peace, and crimes against humanity.

This book grew out of a war crimes tribunal on U.S. policy in Central America and the Caribbean, held in New York City in October 1984. Initially convened by the Center for Constitutional Rights, La Raza Legal Alliance, the National Conference of Black Lawyers, and the National Lawyers Guild, the tribunal was sponsored by numerous organizations.

The organizers believed that sufficient preliminary evidence existed to indict the U.S. government on charges of conducting "its foreign policy in Central America and the Caribbean in violation of international and domestic law and accepted customs."* Particularly, the tribunal was interested in the steadily escalating war against Nicaragua; continued U.S. support of repressive governments in Guatemala, El Salvador, and Honduras; and in the invasion and occupation of the island of Grenada.

The tribunal was seen as an important forum for addressing the legality of these actions, because the U.S. Congress and domestic courts had failed to examine them, and because the government seemed to be ignoring the opinions of many U.S. citizens. Finally, in 1984 the United States refused to submit to the jurisdiction of the International Court of Justice — also known as the World Court — when Nicaragua brought charges that U.S. actions there were violating international law.

In addition to examining the legal context of U.S. involvement in the region, the tribunal hoped to present a forum where U.S. citizens and victims of U.S. aggression could document the human suffering caused by U.S. military activities. Lacking any means of enforcing its judgments, the tribunal hoped to "awaken the public conscience of the people of the United States in order to insure that the U.S. government adheres to the fundamental principles of international law and morality." [From the tribunal's "Statement of Purpose" (See Appendix).]

A TWENTIETH CENTURY INSTITUTION

The history of war crimes tribunals goes back to the Preliminary Peace Conference of 1919, which set up a commission of fifteen to inquire into violations of international law chargeable to Germany and her allies during World War I.

---

*From the tribunal's "Statement of Purpose" (see Appendix).

This body, of course, was far overshadowed by the 1946 Nuremberg International Military Tribunal, which tried top leaders of Nazi Germany. The Nuremberg tribunal was an ad hoc military organization established by executive agreement among the United States, France, Great Britain, and the Soviet Union, and was composed of one judge from each country. The tribunal sentenced twelve defendants to death, seven to imprisonment, and acquitted three. An international military tribunal was also convened in Tokyo to try Japanese war criminals.

The trial at Nuremberg marked a new experiment in the attempt to curb war as an instrument of foreign policy. Its principal innovation was to brand aggressive war, or war in violation of treaties or assurances, as an international crime for which individuals were punishable. Although the conduct of belligerents had long been regulated by convention and customs of war — and trial and punishment for violation of these rules was commonplace — this was the first successful attempt to fix responsibility and to punish for the offense of making a particular war.

The Nuremberg tribunal stated as a point of international law the rule that "individuals have international duties which transcend the national obligations of obedience imposed by the individual state." The tribunal thus established that international law has the power both to declare that a particular war is criminal and to punish those who lead their countries into such wars.

In 1966, amid the beginnings of a public outcry that the U.S. war in Vietnam was indeed such a criminal enterprise, the philosopher Bertrand Russell created a committee to investigate alleged U.S. war crimes there. The trials that followed in Stockholm and Copenhagen were designed to have an impact on world opinion. In May 1967 the tribunal found the U.S. government guilty of three international crimes: a war of aggression against Vietnam; infringement on the sovereignty, territorial integrity, and neutrality of Cambodia; and systematic bombing of civilian targets. Seven months later, the tribunal added five more violations of international law: aggression against the people of Cambodia; the use of and experimentation with illegal weapons; inhumane treatment of prisoners of war; inhumane treatment of civilian populations; and genocide against the Vietnamese people.

Similar Vietnam-era tribunals later were held by a variety of organizations. These included the National Veterans' Inquiry (1970), the Winter Soldier Investigation (1971), and the Dellums Ad Hoc Committee Hearings on U.S. War Crimes in Vietnam (1971). These were independent commissions of inquiry established to gather testimony and evidence from Vietnam veterans, active-duty GIs, and others regarding the nature of U.S. policy in Vietnam and to revitalize the antiwar movement. Local commissions in the form of public hearings also were held in communities throughout the United States.

In 1973 and 1974 the Russell Peace Foundation, responding to numerous appeals to investigate repression in Brazil, Chile, and other countries in Latin America, inaugurated a second Russell tribunal. It aimed to cite and denounce proven human-rights violations in those countries, to analyze the causes of repression, and to analyze the international implications of the repression. The tribunal established an international jury and six investigating commissions to hear testimony, review findings, and draw conclusions.

HOW DOES A TRIBUNAL WORK?

In some ways a war-crimes tribunal is set up to look and function like a court. It has a judge or, more often, a panel of judges. One or more lawyers assume the roles of prosecutors. The jurists consider the evidence in light of what they find to be the applicable law and deliver their judgment.

But there are important differences between war-crimes tribunals and official courts of law, especially in the cases of such "people's" proceedings as the Vietnam and Central America tribunals. At Nuremberg defendants and their lawyers were present to defend themselves. But the Central America and Caribbean tribunal did not hear a defense from the accused—the Reagan administration. The organizers did invite Secretary of State George Shultz to attend or send a representative, but he declined.

Nevertheless, the tribunal organizers felt that the government did not need another opportunity to defend itself, because it has been able to present its side of the story almost daily in the news media, while its accusers have had no comparable media access. To a certain extent, the tribunal is designed to help rectify this imbalance.

Since such a tribunal is an alternative institution, with no power to see that its judgments are carried out, its power lies mostly in its ability to publicize the evidence and its findings in an attempt to appeal to public opinion and conscience at home and abroad.

THE WAR CRIMES TRIBUNAL ON CENTRAL AMERICA AND THE CARIBBEAN

The War Crimes Tribunal on Central America and the Caribbean met in public session and heard testimony at Columbia University and at Riverside Church in New York City on October 8 and 9, 1984.

Similar, though smaller scale, inquiries were held in other U.S. cities, including Chicago; San Francisco; Denver; Los Angeles; Newark, New Jersey; Louisville, Kentucky; Austin, Texas; Salinas, California; Orlando, Florida; Seattle, Washington; and Washington, D.C.

The New York Panel of Jurists consisted of:

- Stanley Faulkner (presiding judge), attorney and member of the Law Commission of the 1967 Bertrand Russell International War Crimes Tribunal on Vietnam;
- The Reverend Ben Chavis, deputy director of the Commission for Racial Justice, United Church of Christ;
- Paul O'Dwyer, attorney and former New York City Council president;
- Rosa Parks, civil rights activist whose action initiated the 1955 bus boycott in Montgomery, Alabama;
- Wilma Reveron-Tío, attorney and executive director of the Office of International Information for the Independence of Puerto Rico;
- Doris Turner, president of Local 1199, Hospital and Health Care Employees Union, RWDSU, AFL-CIO;
- The Honorable Bruce McM. Wright, justice of the New York State Supreme Court.

In rendering its judgment, the panel of jurists took into consideration the following legal instruments:

U.S. Instruments
- The U.S. Constitution, article I, § 8
- The Neutrality Act of 1794
- The War Powers Resolution of 1973
- The Boland Amendment
- The Foreign Assistance Act of 1961
- The International Security and Development Cooperation Act of 1981
- The International Financial Institutions Act of 1977
- The Refugee Act of 1980

United Nations or World Court Instruments
- The Charter of the United Nations
- The Statute of the International Court of Justice
- The Universal Declaration of Human Rights (1948)
- The International Covenant on Civil and Political Rights (1966)
- The International Covenant on Economic, Social and Cultural Rights (1966)
- United Nations General Assembly resolutions 2131, 2625, 3281, 37/184, 37/185, 38/7, 38/10, 38/100, and 38/101
- The Convention on the Prevention and Punishment of the Crime of Genocide (1948)
- The official reports of the trials of war criminals before the Nuremburg International Military Tribunal
- The Geneva Accords of 1949
- The Additional Protocols of 1977 to the Geneva Accords of 1949
- The Hague Conventions of 1899 and 1907 on the Uses and Customs of War
- The Convention Relating to the Status of Refugees (1951)
- The Protocol Relating to the Status of Refugees (1967)
- The General Agreement on Tariffs and Trade

Regional Instruments
- The Charter of the Organization of American States
- The American Declaration of the Rights and Duties of Man (1948)
- The American Convention on Human Rights (1969)
- The Inter-American Treaty of Reciprocal Assistance (1947)
- The Treaty of the Organization of Eastern Caribbean States (1981)

A twelve-member legal secretariat gathered the applicable law, drew up the legal basis for the indictment (which is included in the Appendix), and presented the witnesses. The secretariat also helped the jurists write the findings of fact and conclusions of law.

The tribunal heard sixteen hours of testimony from a total of thirty-seven witnesses and received as exhibits extensive documentation in the form of photographs, reports, articles, and affidavits. The panel also made reference to a number of books and articles in the public domain in weighing the evidence.

Based on this entire body of evidence, the panel of jurists rendered its findings of fact and conclusions of law regarding the compliance of the Reagan administration with domestic and international law. On November 15, 1984, the tribunal delivered its findings to the United Nations Center for Human Rights.

This book presents the statements of twenty-six of the witnesses, along with the findings of fact and conclusions of law. The jurists and members of the legal secretariat had an opportunity to ask questions of the witnesses, but their statements represent the core of what they had to say, and so we have retained only these here for the sake of brevity. The statements have been edited where necessary for clarity, consistency, accuracy, and length.

HISTORICAL BACKGROUND

The bulk of the judgment addresses events of the last few decades and, more particularly, the last few years. The tribunal's investigation, however, made clear that in order to understand the contemporary situation more fully, it is necessary to review briefly the history of U.S. relations with the Central American and Caribbean region. [Editors' note: The section that follows was taken from the testimony of Hazel Ross.]

From very early on, even before the public proclamation of the Monroe Doctrine in 1823, U.S. leaders believed that the United States was destined to play a dominant role in this hemisphere. The various Latin American countries, which had recently cut their colonial ties to Spain, were smaller and weaker than this country, and the U.S. government did not feel compelled to deal with them as equal sovereign states. Rather, a pattern developed of U.S. military intervention to protect U.S. business interests.

Although significant incidents of military intervention began as far back as the middle of the nineteenth century, the most intense period of overt military intervention took place between 1898 and 1934. U.S. troops invaded Cuba four times and stayed for a total of thirteen years. The U.S. military occupied Nicaragua and Haiti for twenty years each and the Dominican Republic for eight. There were additional interventions in Panama, Honduras, and Puerto Rico.

Major General Smedley D. Butler of the U.S. Marine Corps once summarized his role in the hemisphere in the following fashion:

> I spent 33 years and 4 months in active service as a member of our country's most agile military force—the Marine Corps. I spent most of my time being a high-class muscleman for big business, for Wall Street, and for bankers. Thus, I helped make Mexico safe for American oil interests in 1914. I helped make Haiti and Cuba a decent place for National City Bank boys to collect revenues in. I helped purify Nicaragua for the international banking house of Brown Brothers in 1909. I brought light to the Dominican Republic for American sugar interests in 1916. I helped make Honduras right for American fruit companies in 1903. [Greene, Felix. *The Enemy*. New York: Vintage Books (1970), p. 106.]

Over the last 150 years, the United States has participated in more than eighty instances of military intervention in this hemisphere. In view of the fact that contemporary U.S. military involvement in the region is frequently justified as a response to purported Soviet and Cuban interventionism, it is instructive to note that a number of these earlier U.S. interventions took place before the Russian Revolution in 1917, and all of them took place before the Cuban Revolution in 1959.

Direct military intervention was often followed by the installation and support of military dictators who relied on local armies trained by the United States. The most notorious example was the Somoza dynasty in Nicaragua (1936–79).

Whatever the form of U.S. intervention, it has consistently been exercised to install or support governments which had as their constituencies the local oligarchies and U.S. financial interests—governments dedicated to repressing any significant economic or political reform. Two more recent examples of U.S. interventions resulting in brutally repressive regimes are the CIA-sponsored coups in Guatemala in 1954 and in Chile in 1973. Some thirty thousand people have been killed under Pinochet, who has ruled Chile since 1973, and between fifty thousand and one hundred thousand people have been killed by the military regimes that have ruled Guatemala since 1954.

In recent decades U.S. economic intervention in Central America and the Caribbean has been, if anything, more insidious than U.S. military intervention in the area. Massive infusions of foreign capital, in part by foreign investors and in part by large banks competing aggressively to loan their excess capital, have destroyed the traditional agricultural economies in the area. Typical results of such capital invasions include massive social and economic disruption, inflation of land values, displacement of rural populations, destruction of traditional bases of self-sufficiency, and acute economic dependence on foreign capital, imported food, and international markets.

Intervention on Trial

El Salvador

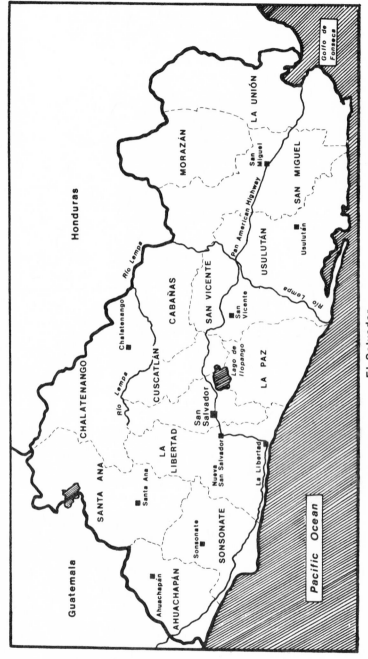

Findings of Fact

El Salvador, a small and densely populated country, has close to five million people in an area the size of Massachusetts. The main economic activity historically has been the cultivation of coffee for export. The majority of the population suffers from severe poverty, along with its frequent concomitant deficiencies in health, education, and life opportunities. This problem of people without economic resources has been festering since at least 1880, when the landed oligarchy abolished the traditional institution of communal lands.

For decades the country was run by and for the plantation owners, a small group of people of European descent traditionally referred to as the "Fourteen Families." Popular unrest broke out during the Great Depression, culminating in a rebellion led by Farabundo Martí in 1932, which was brutally crushed by the army in a massacre in which between ten thousand and thirty thousand Salvadorans were killed. The military officer responsible for the massacre then ruled the country for the next thirteen years.

The period between 1945 and 1979 was characterized by some economic modernization but little economic or political reform. In 1972 and 1977 a few political parties campaigned for moderate reform, but military candidates, through the use of widespread corruption, stole both elections. Political instability forced the United States and the military to overthrow the general whom they had placed in office in 1977 in a bloodless military coup on October 15, 1979. These fraudulent elections, together with a campaign of military repression of all political opposition, led to the formation of various guerrilla groups, which in 1980 formed the Farabundo Martí Front for National Liberation (FMLN). At the same time disenchanted politicians, professionals, and former civilian government officials—all of whom are currently in exile—formed the Democratic Revolutionary Front (FDR),

3

which performs the diplomatic and political functions of the FDR–FMLN coalition.

The last five years have seen a dramatic escalation in the level of repression by forces identified with the government, in the level of revolutionary struggle by the guerrillas, and in the level of U.S. support for and sponsorship of the Salvadoran government.

Repression of all types of political participation and opposition has been characteristic of El Salvador for decades, but it has intensified drastically since the October 1979 coup. Opposition politicians, from President José Napoleón Duarte's Christian Democratic party (PDC) and from the FDR have been disappeared and been murdered, and PDC party activists have frequently been harassed. Labor leaders have been disappeared and murdered or tortured and detained for as long as four years without being charged or tried. Newspaper offices have been violently shut down by the security forces, and papers that are allowed to continue publishing have learned to avoid mentioning the political opposition. Student groups and the academic community have suffered severe persecution, and the National University of El Salvador campus was shut down for four years. The church has also fallen victim to such attacks, most notably when Archbishop Oscar Romero was assassinated while saying mass in March 1980.

Much of this repression has been carried out by "death squads" or by unidentified armed persons. International human-rights observers agree that government security forces are responsible for the overwhelming bulk of this activity. Moreover, except in the few instances where massive campaigns of international pressure have been mounted (for example, in the case of four U.S. churchwomen who were killed), the Salvadoran government has shown no interest in the investigation or prosecution of those responsible for these abuses.

The Salvadoran government, by its ongoing pattern of brutal repression of political opposition, left the opposition no recourse but armed struggle and thus is responsible for the very existence of the current war. Moreover, the Salvadoran government and military have conducted their war against the guerrilla forces in an indiscriminate and inhumane manner. They routinely torture and kill captured guerrillas instead of adhering to the international norms for the treatment of prisoners of war.

The Salvadoran government is waging war against large sectors of its own civilian population, against people who have not taken up arms against the government. As part of its effort to isolate the guerrillas from any civilian bases of support, the Salvadoran military routinely bombs and attacks civilian areas. These attacks are often designed to pressure the people to leave their homes and move to government-controlled villages or refugee camps, or to terrorize them and convince them not to help the guerrillas.

Reprisals against the civilian population are similar to those engaged in by the Nazis. In one incident in July 1984, in villages near Cinquera, Cabañas, Salvadoran troops killed over sixty-five unarmed civilians, over two dozen of whom were under twelve years of age, because their villages had purportedly been used by the FMLN as a staging area for attacking a dam.

The Salvadoran military often declares certain areas free-fire zones, based on their decision that any civilians remaining in the area are supporting the guerrillas and are therefore legitimate targets of military attack. Often the military has killed everybody it found in a village, even though the victims were mothers and children and elderly persons.

At times this campaign against the civilian population has targeted specifically humanitarian activities. In early 1984 the Salvadoran Air Force had a practice of bombing areas where people had gathered to receive assistance from the Red Cross, and one refugee camp in El Salvador has been bombed two times.

The Salvadoran military, by bombing and attacking the civilian population, has created a massive population of internal refugees or displaced persons. The Salvadoran government and military have failed to honor their humanitarian obligation to these displaced persons and have detained, "disappeared," and tortured humanitarian personnel who are attempting to help them.

The Salvadoran government is responsible for the disappearances, torture, and deaths of over forty thousand civilians. That figure constitutes 0.8 percent of the population and would be comparable to 1,750,000 civilian deaths in a country the size of the United States.

The United States provides massive amounts of funding and weapons, as well as training and direction, to the Salvadoran military and massive economic aid to the Salvadoran government. The United States has spent over 570 million dollars in military aid and over a billion dollars to support the Salvadoran government over the last five years. [Editors' note: By the end of 1985 this figure had reached a total of 1.835 billion dollars.]

The United States is providing aerial reconnaissance for the Salvadoran military, which results in the indiscriminate bombing and killing of civilians. U.S. pilots in spotter planes use infrared equipment to detect concentrations of body heat in the Salvadoran countryside. These data are then transmitted to the Pentagon and analyzed, and within two hours attack plans are communicated to the Salvadoran Air Force.

The United States has supplied white phosphorus rockets, which the Salvadoran military is using to conduct chemical warfare against its civilian population. A U. S. doctor who worked in Guazapa for three months saw over two hundred people wounded by phosphorus burns, burns that are almost untreatable in rural El Salvador and therefore often fatal. The Salvadoran military has used napalm and antipersonnel fragmentation devices against the civilian population.

The United States has sent at least fifty-five members of its armed forces to El Salvador, some of whom at times accompany the Salvadoran military during its incursions. The United States has trained over four thousand Salvadoran soldiers and officers, and the troops and officers trained by the United States are often involved in the most notorious human-rights abuses and humanitarian-law violations.

For example, the U.S.-trained Atlacatl Battalion has frequently been responsible for massacres of unarmed villagers. In addition, notwithstanding the U.S. government's attempt to distance itself from the Salvadoran death squads, those death squads grew out of organizations initially set up in the 1960s with CIA support and training. Moreover, the Reagan administration's December 1983 publicity campaign against the death squads focused on individual officers and ignored the more important role played by the security organizations to which those officers belonged.

[Editors' note: In 1986 the United States began unrestricted training of Salvadoran paramilitary security units following the lifting of a decade-old congressional ban on such aid. The five million dollar program marked a sharp increase in training compared with help extended under several previous special exemptions granted by Congress. Many of the officers being trained came from units suspected of contributing members to the death squads.]

Over eight hundred thousand refugees have fled El Salvador for fear of being harmed by the repression and the hostilities. Over three hundred thousand have sought refuge in the United States. The United States has ignored its humanitarian obligations to these refugees, refusing to grant them political asylum or even extended voluntary departure, and has forcibly repatriated over thirty-five thousand of them to El Salvador. Some of those who returned have been tortured and killed.

Background to the Crisis

Testimony of Robert Armstrong

Executive Director of the North American Congress on Latin America and co-author of El Salvador: The Face of Revolution.

The civil war in El Salvador in the 1980s is a result of two things that happened during the 1970s: Segments of the populace organized and called for reform, and the government reacted to those calls with repression.

The reform movements of the 1970s were not the first groups in the history of El Salvador to protest against a system that benefited primarily the "Fourteen Families," the rich land-owning families who dominated the country's economy and government. There were peasant revolts at the end of the nineteenth century, massive political mobilization during and after World War II, and turbulent trade-union activity during the 1920s.

In 1932 peasants, workers, students, and even some soldiers banded together under Farabundo Martí and other members of the Communist party and tried to overthrow the dictatorship of General Maximiliano Hernández Martínez. The military quashed the rebels with little effort and went on to massacre as many as thirty thousand people in retribution.

When Martínez finally fell in 1944, there was a renewed popular struggle. In the 1950s trade unions battled for recognition. In the 1960s student groups challenged governmental authority, and opposition political parties began to garner significant support.

In the early 1970s the popular struggle achieved new levels of consciousness and unity. The Salvadoran economy took a dramatic turn for the worse, and many believed that their situation would not improve unless the structure of the economy was radically altered. Liberation theology gave many Christians a new sense of their worth and their right to band together to fight injustice. In this process many Salvadoran workers and peasants underwent profound transformations — personal, political, and ultimately spiritual — and acquired a new sense of their power as actors in the political arena.

7

The country's rulers – the land-owning oligarchy and its servant and ally, the military – could have responded to this development by opening up the political process to wider popular participation and by permitting some economic reforms. Instead, their response was to try to silence the cries for reform.

Peaceful demonstrations were crushed violently. Activists in all branches of the popular movement – religious professionals, lay parish leaders, student leaders, labor union activists, teachers, and other professionals – were taken from their homes or offices, detained for long periods (without charges, trials, or help from lawyers), disappeared, tortured, and murdered. First directed against the activists themselves, this campaign quickly extended to their families and even their friends and associates. Whole families have been slaughtered or driven into exile.

The U.S. government's reaction to this repression of the popular movement has been to brand the popular struggle as communist and Soviet-dominated, and to support the government (the wealthy minority) and the military in their attempt to silence the cries for justice and change.

Before 1979 the United States had traditionally had very little involvement with El Salvador. Compared to the large investments by U.S. corporations in Guatemala and Honduras, our economic involvement in El Salvador has been minimal. Similarly, our national security concerns have led to deeper involvements elsewhere in Central America and little of this attention has been directed toward El Salvador.

Our level of involvement has changed dramatically in the last five years. Since 1979 the U.S. government has provided 570 million dollars in military aid and 1.15 billion dollars in economic assistance to the Salvadoran government, extraordinarily high sums for a country of under five million people.

We have trained some four thousand Salvadoran soldiers and provided the Salvadoran military with a wide range of lethal weaponry – all the way from A-37 Dragonflies and Huey helicopters to M-16 rifles. We have over fifty military advisers on the ground in El Salvador training and advising the Salvadoran Army and Air Force, and other military personnel flying over the country and providing crucial intelligence data.

But the U.S. involvement in El Salvador is not limited to military assistance. U.S. advisers are in daily contact with all branches of the government in El Salvador, offering financial aid, technical assistance, and advice on the conduct of government affairs. U.S. diplomats also lobby in the international arena for financial assistance to El Salvador. Without U.S. financial support, the Salvadoran economy would collapse in short order, and the government would cease functioning.

In addition to prolonging the war, the United States' strong support of the current regime in El Salvador will lead to a long-term commitment to that regime that will be difficult to back away from. We have chosen sides in this struggle, and we have become committed to a military defeat of the rebel forces. To achieve that defeat, we might easily have to send in U.S. combat troops and become involved in a replay of the Vietnam War. It's hard to see such a result being in the best interests of the United States or the people of El Salvador.

Torture, Summary Executions, and Government Prisons

Testimony of Ramón Flores

Salvadoran medical student, former prisoner, and torture victim.

My name is Ramón Flores, and I am from El Salvador. I was a university student, a medical student, until the university closed in 1980. At that stage in my life, with the background I had in medical studies, I felt it was important to put that experience to some practical use for the people of my country. That is why my wife and I decided to work in the refugee camps that were supported by the church. (By "the church" I mean the new church in El Salvador, the church that was inspired by our beloved and revered Archbishop Monsignor Romero.) In the center refugees were given some protection. They were given some food and some attention.

So we joined. We incorporated ourselves into the work of the refugee camps. I began work as a paramedic in the camps, and my wife worked as a health educator among the children there. We worked in the camps about two and a half years.

Basically, the people in the camps were refugees who had fled the zones where there was conflict. They were a product of the war, of the conflict, of the bombings and the strafing by the air force. We began to see many children, women, and old people arriving. They were basically the people who came to the refuge.

It became difficult to provide sufficient aid for these refugees. The church began to ask for aid from abroad. They asked for medicine, clothing, and food. International delegations began to arrive.

Many delegations arrived from North American churches. Baptist, Mennonite, Lutheran, and other churches sent delegations. They provided a great deal of help, and at the same time they acquired a complete picture of the consequences of the aggression, of the consequences of these constant attacks upon the towns, upon the people.

This naturally did not please the government. They began to arrest people who worked in the refugee centers. They killed some. Many, many disappeared, and many of us who did such work ended up in jail.

For example, the church that I worked for had a full quota of refugees. All of us who were working with them were captured and taken prisoner: the pastor of the church, two doctors, myself, who was working as a paramedic, two technicians, agricultural specialists, and also the people who were teaching catechism to the children. We were all accused of collaborating with the guerrillas.

This is the most frightening part of all. So that you get an idea of what it's like, let me tell you that one night in June 1983 armed men came to my house and captured me and my wife and children. Can you imagine accusing a six-year-old, a three-year-old, and a three-month-old infant of collaborating with the guerrillas? When we were captured, we were immediately blindfolded, so it was difficult for us to get a sense of exactly what was happening at the time.

It's very important for you to understand that the captures that take place in my country are generally carried out by persons not wearing uniforms, using vehicles without license plates and without identification. Even the arms they use are not arms that are normally used by the army or the security forces. They are usually carried out late at night. All of this is to create confusion, so that no one who sees an arrest can give a description.

I was taken to a private house, and my wife and children were taken to a barracks on a military base. After eight days my children were taken to an adoption center. The center staff were told the children were orphans who had been found abandoned in the street. We would never have found out where the children were had it not been for the coincidence that a neighbor of ours happened to be doing some social work in this center.

I was held in the private house for five days by the paramilitary, and I was subjected to torture, physical torture as well as psychological torture. The tortures they generally apply to any political prisoner are pretty much the same. But depending on the significance they attach to the particular prisoner, they may apply different combinations of torture.

For example, electrical shocks are applied to different parts of the body. It all depends on how much damage they are willing to inflict on a particular prisoner. For example, there are electric shocks to the ears, to the lower part of the abdomen, as well as to the genitals. I was subjected to electrical shocks to the ears.

There is also the famous "little plane with the pilot." It consists of being suspended by the arms, with your arms held up by ropes, while a man gets on top of you and jumps on you.

Then there are just the beatings and the stranglings. There are torture sessions where you're surrounded by various torturers and they take turns doing their favorite torture.

For me, I think the tortures that leave the most damage are the psychic tortures. There are moments when one thinks it would be better for them to kill you.

In one torture, they take a captive's blindfold off and take you into a room. One of the torturers comes in with blood all over him and says, "Well, is this the next one I have to kill? My previous victim, the one I just killed, was hardly any trouble. I am ready for this one."

My wife and I have experienced these psychic tortures. I have suffered them in relation to my wife and children. I still bear the scars of this torture. Any political prisoner is subjected to these practices.

Every time someone is arrested with a family group, full advantage is taken of that situation. The family becomes a tool for applying pressure to the individual: for example, for getting the individual to make a public confession or to make a videotape in which he or she says, for example, that there are Cubans or Nicaraguans fighting among the insurgents. That type of thing. So the relatives are used to apply pressure. This is a practice they have already used and one that they will probably continue to use.

Many times the children are lost. I had three companions when I was in prison that this happened to. One of them does not know what happened to one of his children. The second does not know what happened to two of his children, and the third does not know what happened to any of his children. All of these children were arrested at exactly the same times that their parents were.

The truth is that the children do not spend a very long time at these centers. The friend who told us about our children also told us that the children are sometimes taken away very soon. Sometimes they are only there for a couple of days, and the family never hears from them again. The children are adopted, and the families that adopt them are North American.

After those five days in the private house, where they were torturing me, they moved me to the military base where my wife was being held, and we were both held there for a while. For over twenty days we were in the category of disappeared persons. None of the official organizations, such as the International Red Cross or the human-rights organizations, were able to locate us during this time.

Under those circumstances, especially when one is taken to a private home rather than an official building, you realize that since you haven't been identified to the authorities, it's easy for them to kill you and dump you along the roadside. You appear as another victim of the death squads.

But thanks to God, they made a mistake when they picked us up and left a clue indicating that we were in the hands of the authorities. So after twenty-three days at the military base, I was transferred to Mariona Prison.

There are three things they can do to a person who is being held secretly. They can either make you disappear, kill you, or transfer you to an official detention facility, where human-rights organizations can locate you. Which alternative they choose depends on the attention or the publicity that has been generated about the particular case.

So when you consider the alternatives, one is really lucky to be transferred to a prison such as Mariona. I don't say that because Mariona Prison is a nice place to be. It isn't. But the significance of being a prisoner there is that it increases one's chances of getting out of the situation alive.

I was held in Mariona Prison for eleven months. I might have spent more time there, because in Mariona Prison a political prisoner does not serve a determinate sentence. Usually no official charges have been filed against him, and he is not facing any particular judicial proceedings. One is just held indefinitely. After eleven months in Mariona, I was set free, but only after I had paid a large sum of money to a military judge. Every prisoner has to pay a price to be freed.

In Mariona I was told that the charges against me were that I had provided medical services to the guerrillas of the FMLN. I demanded that they present me with proof of their charges, and I later asked the judge to provide me with some proof to substantiate these charges, but they couldn't. The real purpose of my arrest, and of the arrests of people like me, was to disrupt and intimidate the groups that were providing services to the refugee centers.

Salvadoran government authorities prefer people to leave El Salvador rather than stay in the country and live in refugee centers. If the people leave the country, the government can say that they are just economic migrants and not really refugees. To have the refugee camps inside El Salvador is dangerous for the government, because it is a proof to the world of the consequences of the war.

Conditions in El Salvador are not better now under Duarte. They are worse. There are constant bombings in the provinces of San Vicente and Morazan, and many women and children are being killed. There are still bodies found on the streets of downtown San Salvador. The only difference is that they no longer have signs on them saying that the executions were carried out by the death squads. Some of the papers have gone so far as to say that these murders were the result of crimes of passion, but this is absurd.

Repression of the Trade Unions

Testimony of Héctor Recinos, Jr.

Son of a leader of the union of Salvadoran hydroelectric workers (STECEL).

[*Editors' note*: At the time of the tribunal, Héctor Recinos's father had been imprisoned along with nine other Salvadoran hydroelectrical union (STECEL) workers for over four years without access to counsel and without having formal charges filed against them. The unionists had been rounded up and detained in August 1980 while participating in a general strike called to protest the intensifying government repression. Due largely to Hector's efforts and to an organized campaign by U.S. and European trade unionists, President Duarte, within hours of Hector's testimony before this tribunal, announced that a military judge had ordered his father and the rest of "the STECEL 10" released.]

My name is Héctor Recinos. I am sixteen years old. I have been in the United States for seven months. I fled El Salvador and came to the United States with my two younger brothers, Luís Eduardo, who is eight, and Jaime Alberto, who is fourteen.

My father belongs to STECEL, the union of workers in the company that generates electricity for El Salvador. In August 1980 the union declared a work stoppage. They demanded that 360 workers who have been fired be allowed to return to their jobs. They also made demands for justice on behalf of eight members of the union who had been assassinated by the government's security forces.

While they were on strike, they were surrounded by members of the National Guard, the national police, and the army. They were taken to the National Guard headquarters and then to the prison in Santa Tecla and, finally, to Mariona Prison in San Salvador.

During their four years in prison, they have been subjected to torture. They have even been filmed during these torture sessions, as if it were a pleasurable event for the torturers. During these four years no

14

charges have been brought against them, nor have they been brought before any tribunal.

One day in 1982 my mother, who was working with the Committee of Relatives of the Disappeared and of Political Prisoners, was taken out of our house along with my thirteen-year-old sister by sixteen heavily armed men in civilian clothes. I was playing in the street at the time. When I saw them entering the house without asking permission, I was worried about the safety of my younger brothers, so we tried to leave the neighborhood, but one of the men called to us, and we had to stay.

I was fourteen years old at the time, my brother Jaime was eleven, and my brother Luís was six. We had been playing with a friend of Luís, and we went to that friend's house. We spent two hours there. Then one of the neighbors came by and told us that all the lights were out in our house and it was quiet. We stayed that night at that friend's house, and the next day we went to our grandmother's house. I have never been back to our home.

My grandmother's house was about forty-five minutes away. When we got there, we had to work in order to support ourselves and help our grandmother; so we got a job in a factory that makes floor tiles. We earned nine dollars a week working in that factory. We worked there from August 1982 to the end of that year.

Toward the end of the year, I asked my younger brothers if they wanted to go to school, and they said yes. The first school we tried to register at said they couldn't take us because we were the children of a trade-union leader, and our being students in that school would put the other students' lives in danger. But after we adopted false names, we were able to go to school.

It was under those false names that we were able to visit our father in prison for the first time after our mother and sister were captured. Since our father was a well known trade-union leader, it was too risky for us to appear at the prison and give our real names.

By that time we had received a letter from our cousin in Los Angeles. The cousin said we should come to the United States, because there wasn't anyone in El Salvador to take care of us. When we spoke about this to our father in prison, he said it was a good idea, because he had no idea how we had been getting along without any family during that time. He agreed that we should come to the United States.

On December 30, 1983, we crossed the border illegally from El Salvador to Guatemala. That part of the border is a river. We pretended to swim in the river and went over to the other side. Our grandfather was waiting for us on the other side. He had been advised that we were coming and had arranged to meet us after we crossed the border. My grandfather had a horse with him. We put my younger brother on the horse, and the rest of us walked to my grandfather's house, which is about four hours from the border.

We spent a month with my grandfather on his farm in Guatemala. He is seventy-five years old, but he is still working the land. We helped him out for a month.

On February 4, 1984, we left Guatemala en route to the United States, crossing the border from Guatemala to Mexico the same way we had crossed the border to leave El Salvador. It took us another five days to cross Mexico and reach the U.S. border.

We entered the United States at Calexico, California. It was about 11:00 at night. We soon saw some immigration patrol cars, so we had to duck down and hide in a ditch alongside the road. At first the immigration patrol pointed their lights above our heads and didn't see us, but the third time they came by, they saw us and arrested us. They set a bond of two thousand dollars on each of us.

The next day they transferred us to San Diego. There I got in touch with El Rescate, a group of affiliated organizations that help refugees. El Rescate got our bonds reduced to five hundred dollars each and helped locate our relatives. Then our family was able to come see us and pay the bond. That is how we got out.

Since then we have been doing what my father told me we should do. He said that when we got to a country that has free expression, we should speak for him, because he had not committed any crime. He said it was no crime to stand up for the rights of workers and their families, and for the rights of the 360 union workers who had been fired, and of the 16 union members who had been killed during this period. He said that it should not be a crime to speak out for them. So that is what we are doing up here.

Sometimes I am afraid that my speaking out on behalf of my father might be putting his life in even more danger, but Duarte speaks of democratic rights, and it should be just for us to make these demands. After four years they should be brought to trial or released.

We have experienced in our flesh and bones the results of the arms that are being sent to El Salvador. We have lived through the same suffering that many thousands of Salvadorans are living through. We need food. We don't need arms. We can't eat bullets.

The Use of Napalm, White Phosphorus, and Other Antipersonnel Weapons: Reprisals Against the Civilian Population

Testimony of Richard Alan White

Project director at the Third World Center for Social and Economic Studies in Mexico City, senior research fellow at the Council on Hemispheric Affairs in Washington, D.C., and author of Paraguay's Autonomous Revolution *and* The Morass: United States Intervention in Central America.

My testimony today will focus on two of the more alarming aspects of the war in El Salvador: the greatly intensified air war and Nazi-style reprisals carried out against the civilian population.

There are a number of features of air war that I would like to discuss with you. The most serious is the fact that the Salvadoran military is attacking civilian targets.

I brought with me today photographs that I took in the village of Miramundo in Chalatenango province. The photographs show the ruins of people's homes. These homes are civilian targets, and the destruction resulted from direct hits by bombs during an air attack on September 4, 1984. The only bombs dropped during the attack directly hit houses or landed right next to them. That is to say, this destruction of nonmilitary targets and the accompanying civilian casualties were not random or accidental. They were the deliberate results of precision bombing.

We talked to the inhabitants and learned that the bombing attack occurred early in the morning without warning. There had not been any recent military activity in the area. The Dragonflies just flew in at 7:30 one morning and started dropping their bombs.

Miramundo is hardly an isolated instance. Attacks on civilian targets are almost an inevitable component of a military campaign of counterinsurgency.

Counterinsurgency theorists realize that the strength of a guerrilla insurgency arises from its relationship to the civilian population. The governments facing guerrilla movements are usually repressive and unpopular. Almost by definition they have a hard time winning over the people's hearts and minds, which they attempt to do in order to undercut popular support and isolate the guerrillas. Counterinsurgency theory is the military solution to this political problem. It advises the government to relocate the rural population into fortified settlements subject to government control. Since the peasants normally don't want to leave their homes and live under government control, the government must use military force and terror to make them do this.

That is a large part of what military counterinsurgency strategy in El Salvador is about: air attacks and ground troop sweeps through "contested areas," areas where government control is not secure; attacking villages, destroying homes, burning crops, massacring the civilians, and tearing apart the social fabric; causing people to leave their villages and run for their lives, fleeing through the mountains and the jungle for months without food or medicine until they can flee no more, until they are prostrate, until they give up running and turn themselves in to the authorities and live as refugees in the relocation centers run by the government and the military.

Once the people are in the relocation centers or resettled in the "reconstructed areas," which resemble the "strategic hamlets" from the Vietnam era, they are subject to extensive government control. Forbidden to leave and reenter the controlled areas freely, they are required to participate in civic-action projects, which are designed and funded by the U.S. Agency for International Development and called "humanitarian aid" by our government.

This aspect of counterinsurgency — the deliberate creation of refugees on a massive scale — does not happen without the use of widespread military force and terror. This constitutes a violation of the 1949 Geneva Conventions, which prohibit military campaigns against civilians even when those civilians perform some support functions for opposition military forces.

The Salvadoran military's air war against its own civilian population is right now in the process of escalating significantly, because the United States has just decided to furnish El Salvador with AC-47s. The AC-47, or Armored Cargo-47, is a military version of a DC-3 aircraft but has larger fuel tanks and an extended station time. Known during the Vietnam era as "Puff the Magic Dragon," the AC-47 can stay aloft circling the battleground for six hours.

The AC-47 is normally fitted with three synchronized electronic Gatling guns. Using an infrared sighting device, the pilot can fire eighteen thousand rounds a minute. Congressional objection to this escalation led to a compromise agreement that the administration would deliver only one plane for the time being and would replace the Gatling guns with .50-caliber machine guns. Although these guns fire fewer rounds per minute than the Gatling guns (only fifteen hundred), they still represent a significant escalation in the Salvadoran military's firepower. The introduction of even the modified AC-47 represents a new and more deadly level of warfare technology, a level never before seen in Central America.

There are two other aspects of the air war that I want to comment on today, and both of them constitute violations of humanitarian norms of war. One is the use of antipersonnel weapons, and the other is the use of chemical weapons — napalm and white phosphorus.

Along with numerous testimonies from victims, I have first-hand evidence that the Salvadoran military is in fact using antipersonnel bombs. During my various trips to El Salvador over the past years, I had repeatedly asked U.S. ambassadors, U.S. military advisers, and Salvadoran military commanders if the Salvadoran armed forces ever used antipersonnel devices. These people had consistently assured me that this never happened. Then in May I went to El Salvador as an unofficial observer of the elections. Instead of my usual press credential, I had an observer's pass, so for the weekend of the elections I could go anywhere I wanted and the army wouldn't stop me.

I heard that government forces had just attacked a guerrilla column with aerial bombardment and artillery shelling near the town of Ilobasco in the province of Cabañas, so I went there. After checking on the voting, I asked several army officers if there had been any recent fighting in the area. They all said no. Later, as I was walking along the main street, a man who was walking alongside of me pulled on my shirt. I looked over at him. He kept his gaze straight ahead, but he quietly asked me, "What do you want to know?" "Where was the fighting the day before yesterday?" I asked. "Out at the turn to the mines," he replied. I asked him how to get there, and he told me which roads to take.

I followed the man's directions, and a CBS news team followed me. We came to a military roadblock and were ordered to turn back. I took advantage of my status as an election observer. "Listen," I said, "I am a delegate here, and I want to see if the people there are able to come in and vote. If you don't let me through, I will report your interference to the National Electoral Commission, and it will cause a national scandal and reflect poorly on the democratic process, and you will suffer the consequences!" So the captain let me through, but the news team had to stay behind.

I found the hamlet where the bombing and shelling had occurred. Four houses were destroyed. Trees had been blown apart. There were bomb craters, and a series of small holes in the ground on the hillside that looked like the result of machine-gun strafing from an airplane.

The farmers came out and talked with me. I pointed to the holes and said, "Look at the machine-gun strafings." They responded, "No, those holes were not made by a machine gun. They were made by a bomb that explodes above the ground." I questioned that, so they took out their machetes and dug out from the holes a couple of white metal bomb fragments, which they gave to me. They were right. The holes had been made by an antipersonnel fragmentation device called a pineapple bomb. It's a bomb that is specifically designed to wound and kill people, rather than destroy structures or military equipment. I will leave with the tribunal this bomb fragment that the farmers dug out of their fields as evidence that they are right, and the U.S. and Salvadoran officials wrong, about the use of antipersonnel devices.

The other specific violation of humanitarian warfare norms that I have been able to document is the use of chemical warfare in the form of napalm and white-phosphorus incendiary devices. I visited El Salvador last month as part of a delegation sponsored by Medical Aid to El Salvador. One of the goals of the delegation was to investigate the charges that the Salvadoran military has been using napalm and white phosphorus against the civilian population. We were able to confirm these charges in two ways—by interviewing witnesses and by examining survivors.

We talked with refugees who had fled contested areas and asked them about the different kinds of weapons employed by the air force. We were careful not to use leading questions, and we never introduced any technical names like "napalm." Only a few of the refugees used the term "napalm"; none referred to "phosphorus." Mostly, they just described what they had seen.

They spoke of a bomb or rocket that exploded into bits of "white fire" that could not be extinguished. They explained how a piece of it embedded in your arm or leg would just go on burning for hours. Even if you smothered the wound with mud for a couple of days, when the mud was finally removed the fire would start up and burn all over again. All these characteristics are unique to white-phosphorus burns.

Their description of napalm was just as accurate. They told us that the "fire bombs" didn't make a big hole in the ground (as explosives do), that they spew off enormous clouds of black smoke, and that their gummy substance sticks to you so that you can't wipe it off and burns you terribly. Around forty people told us of seeing such attacks.

One of the members of our delegation was Dr. John Constable, a burn specialist at Massachusetts General Hospital who dealt with napalm victims during the Vietnam era. We were able to locate three people who had suffered napalm burns and managed to survive. Dr. Constable examined these victims and was able to confirm—for the first time that I know of in the Salvadoran conflict—that they were in fact victims of a napalm attack. I brought photographs of the people Dr. Constable examined, and I will now pass them to the judges.

I should comment briefly on the fact that we found only three victims, which might sound like a very small number. For one thing, napalm victims in an underdeveloped country rarely survive. Without immediate and skilled medical attention, a napalm or phosphorus victim usually dies of dehydration, infection, or phosphorus poisoning. Dr. Constable toured forty-three of the forty-four provincial hospitals in Vietnam in 1967, when napalm use was at its height, and found only twelve burn victims.

An additional factor is the Salvadoran government's desire to cover up their use of napalm. Napalm victims who come to government-controlled areas do not stay in circulation long. They disappear, because they are living evidence of the crimes being committed by the government.

The second major topic that I want to discuss with you today is the Nazi-style reprisals that the Salvadoran military has carried out against the civilian population. I want to tell you about a massacre that happened just a few months ago on July 21 and 22, 1984, in San Antonio, Guiliguiste, and seven other neighboring towns in the northwestern portion of the province of Cabañas.

I have pieced this story together from a number of different sources: interviews I conducted with peasants who lived there; newspaper articles; Socorro Juridico, a human rights organization; Tutela Legal, the archbishop's legal aid office; and a letter from Father Rutilio Sánchez, who practices his ministry in that region, which is a contested area, and who is obviously sympathetic to the rebel cause.

On June 28 the FMLM guerrilla forces attacked the nearby Cerrón Grande Dam, a major source of electric power and heavily guarded by the military. The attack was one of the most embarrassing defeats the Salvadoran military has suffered to date. The rebels succeeded in inflicting damage to this key strategic position, and they killed over a hundred government troops.

Ten days later a guerrilla commander died in battle. In his possession was found the plan the rebel forces had followed in their attack on the dam. The plan described how the FMLN had infiltrated the towns in question, bringing in weapons, ammunition, food, and other supplies in preparation for the attack on the dam.

Preceded by "softening up" operations—mortar shelling and aerial bombardments—the government soldiers began their advance into the area on July 20 in a large semicircular formation originating in the towns of Tejutepeque, Tenancingo, and San José Guayabal. At 3:00 P.M. the next day, July 21, columns of the U.S.-trained Atlacatl Battalion, along with detachments from the 3rd and 5th Infantry divisions, arrived at San Antonio and Guiliguiste.

When government troops come into a town in any of the contested areas, the people run and hide, because they know that they might be killed. One very sad aspect is that the people who are most often caught and killed are disproportionately the people who can't run as fast — the very young and the very old.

True to this grisly pattern, upon arriving at the now-empty towns, the soldiers burned and destroyed houses, barns, and crops in the fields. They then began a systematic machine gunning and mortaring of the surrounding hillsides and gullies where they suspected people might be hiding. Soon they located about three hundred noncombatant civilians — mostly children, their mothers, and old people who were unable to flee to more remote hiding places — clustered in a deep ravine along the banks of the Sucio River. The following description of what happened next is a direct translation from Father Sánchez's letter as told to him by one of the survivors: "From a distance of 500 meters they began to fire. I heard desperate cries, cries for mercy: 'Don't shoot! We are unarmed! We are civilians! We surrender! Don't kill the children!' But the butchering did not stop." The adults had given up hope for their own lives, and were reduced to pleading for the lives of the children. According to Tutela Legal, which requires the most rigorous documentation and has the most conservative figures, sixty-eight people were massacred in these towns on July 21 and 22, and twenty-seven of them were under the age of twelve. The army went on to each of the towns named in the rebel document, and in each town they destroyed homes, burned crops, and killed civilians.

On July 25, a few days after the soldiers left, Father Sánchez celebrated mass in the town of La Escopeta with sixty-five survivors of the massacres and took their testimony. In his words:

> They all coincided in pointing out that the communities that were at-tacked offered no resistance; that there was no guerrilla fighting going on [at that time], not even the presence of the FMLN [guerrilla] army; that [the soldiers] did not accord clemency to anyone; that they took no prisoners; that it is false that they tried to spare women or children; that they raped and later executed the girls; that the men and older boys were shot, some after being tortured.

I visited some of those devastated sites on September 21, two months after the massacres. Hundreds of people used to live in some of those villages, but there's no one there now. The people who survived the attacks have fled. The structures are flattened. The fields are barren. Already vines and other vegetation are beginning to creep over and cover up the rubble. Soon the villages will be reclaimed by the jungle.

Both the United States and El Salvador are signatories to the 1949 Geneva Conventions, which make it a crime to attack unarmed civilian supporters of military groups. Nevertheless, one of the officers involved in the atrocities tried to rationalize the crimes by arguing that the guerrillas realized that there would be "repercussions" for the assault on the Cerrón Grande Dam.

According to the Salvadoran officer's way of thinking, the fact that the people living in these towns sympathized with the insurgent movement was cause enough to justify treating the entire area as a free-fire zone where anyone whom the armed forces found was considered a legitimate target to be killed. As the officer himself put it, "There are no people living in those hamlets. There isn't a dog or a bird of prey. Only terrorists."

As something of a footnote to this tragic episode, because of the press reports concerning the July massacres, President José Napoleón Duarte promised to conduct an official investigation into the matter and bring the guilty to justice. Along with interviewing dozens of survivors in refugee camps, I conducted extensive interviews during two trips to Cabañas province in late September with the local people. I could not find a single person who had even seen a government investigator, and to this day nobody has been charged with the crimes.

The Policy of Displacement and the Flight of Refugees

Testimony of Father Henry Atkins, Jr.

A founder of Witness for Peace, former missionary in Central America, Episcopalian chaplain at Rutgers University and activist in the the sanctuary movement.

In 1981 and 1982 I lived for a period in the camp for Salvadoran refugees located in La Virtud, Honduras, near the border with El Salvador. Reports had been coming out of the camp that Salvadoran soldiers and death-squad members were crossing over the Salvadoran border into Honduras, entering the camp, and taking refugees out and killing them. People at the National Council of Churches felt that these abuses would diminish if some North Americans were there living in the camp, keeping watch over the camp, and confronting the intruders.

The refugees in the camp had come out of great tribulation. When we speak about what has been happening in Central America recently, we use words like "torture" and "murder" so often that sometimes we lose touch with the vicious nature of what these people have suffered. Let me give an example of what these refugees are fleeing from.

When I arrived in La Virtud in December of 1981, the first woman I talked with appeared to be in a trance and had been crying for about twenty-four hours without stopping. Finally, we were able to calm her down and get her to talk. She was from Chalatenango province. She told us that one day Salvadoran soldiers came into her village and accused her seventeen-year-old daughter, who was pregnant, of having slept with a guerrilla. When the daughter denied this charge, the soldier cut open her belly with his bayonet, stuck the fetus on the bayonet point, and fed the fetus to some pigs in the road. Then he poured gasoline all over the young woman's body and forced her mother to set her on fire. If this woman came to the United States, the State Department would no doubt say she is an economic refugee.

Many of the refugees we talked to had been raped. Several of the relief workers in the camp were later tortured and killed. One woman in particular, with whom I worked very closely, was captured and tortured after I left, and is now in a very grave psychological condition.

24

One out of every five Salvadorans has been displaced. Most of these displaced are still in El Salvador, surviving as internal refugees, but many of them have come to the United States.

The 1980 Refugee Act provides that people fleeing political persecution can be granted temporary asylum in this country until it is safe for them to return to their own country. But the present administration has refused to grant this relief to refugees from Guatemala or El Salvador. Acting on State Department recommendations, the Immigration and Naturalization Service (INS) denies over 95 percent of the applications by Salvadoran refugees for political asylum on the grounds that they came here only to get a better salary.

In fact, many Salvadoran and Guatemalan refugees are sent back to their native countries without even going through the asylum application process. At last report, our government was deporting as many as eight hundred Salvadorans and Guatemalans every month. We don't know how many of those refugees have been captured at the airport in San Salvador and tortured or killed, or how many of them were allowed to return to their villages, only then to be arrested, along with those they contacted. But we do know that these things have happened, and we know that most of these people are not coming to the United States mainly to improve their standard of living. They are coming because they fear being injured, raped, tortured, or killed.

Church groups in this country have responded to the plight of the Salvadoran and Guatemalan refugees by forming the sanctuary movement. Over 160 churches and synagogues have declared themselves sanctuaries, and others have declared their support. We do this in spite of the fact that the Reagan administration believes our actions are illegal, and in spite of the fact that the potential criminal penalty for each violation — each time you help a refugee — is two thousand dollars and five years in prison. Thus many of us are facing hundreds of years in jail and hundreds of thousands of dollars in fines. But we are prepared to stand with the Salvadoran and Guatemalan refugees no matter how long they put us in jail.

Some of our people from the sanctuary movement went to Washington, D.C., and met with Elliot Abrams at the State Department. In that meeting Mr. Abrams told us he had a plan to take care of the refugees' fears of persecution in El Salvador. He said we should build a camp in El Salvador surrounded with barbed wire and guarded by U.S. soldiers. Then whenever a Salvadoran refugee being returned to El Salvador fears persecution, that refugee can simply tell a Salvadoran police officer or military officer that he is afraid, and then he would be placed in this camp, where he would be protected from persecution. I don't have the time here to give a detailed critique of this proposal. I hope you agree that it gives a very scary picture of what the Reagan administration has in mind for the refugees.

Health Effects of the War on Women and Children

Testimony of Joanne Palmisano, M.D.

Professor in Department of Internal Medicine, State University of New York, Downstate Medical Center, and member of the Second Public Health Commission delegation to El Salvador in January 1983.

In January 1983 I traveled to Mexico City and San Salvador with six respected U.S. health professionals, three of them fluent in Spanish, to investigate abuses of health rights and medical neutrality in El Salvador. Our trip was sponsored by several U.S. health groups, among them the American Public Health Association.

In Mexico City we met with exiled Salvadoran health officials, many of whom had formerly been affiliated with the medical school or the Ministry of Public Health in El Salvador. In San Salvador we conducted interviews with a large number of government, health, relief, and religious officials and workers. We visited several hospitals, two prisons, and a refugee camp.

Based on our interviews and site inspections, we concluded that there is almost a complete breakdown in the health-care system in El Salvador. The training of health-care personnel is at a near standstill. The health and sanitary conditions of refugees living in San Salvador are appalling. The children of El Salvador are suffering terribly as a result of the militarization of the society.

A severe crisis exists in El Salvador's hospitals. We visited three of the four hospitals in San Salvador and one clinic in a rural suburb of the capital.

At the maternity hospital, two or three women occupied each bed. Women in labor told us they had been unable to obtain prenatal care, including nutritional supplements such as vitamins, milk powder, and cooking oil. The poor general health of these women and the lack of prenatal care account for the high incidence of premature births and other neonatal problems. The death rate of infants admitted to the sick-newborn nursery approaches a staggering 80 percent at this hospital.

The health statistics we obtained from a rural health worker are devastating. He reported an infant mortality rate of 180 per 1,000 live births. In some rural areas 40 percent of newborns weigh less than 2.5 kilograms, the internationally recognized danger point. One third of the population is clinically anemic, and 80 percent of the children under five years of age suffer from malnutrition in terms of both protein and calorie intake.

All the hospitals, including the main public hospital and the military hospital, have severe shortages of food, staff, supplies, blood, and diagnostic equipment. Antibiotics and analgesics are scarce. In general, the wards are overcrowded. The patients have a variety of conditions common to large city hospitals, as well as certain tropical diseases such as amoebiasis, leprosy, malaria, and typhoid fever.

The outpatient hospital pharmacy had no drugs to fill prescriptions. When available, medications, even those distributed by the Ministry of Health, are exorbitantly priced relative to the limited income of most Salvadorans. Nurses and physicians in the operating and recovery rooms noted shortages of anesthesia, oxygen, antibiotics, sutures, and blood.

Although just as crowded as the public hospitals, the military hospital was strikingly different in that it was clean and adequately staffed. There was some sophisticated equipment in the laboratory compared with the antiquated equipment at the main civilian hospital, but we could not ascertain whether the personnel knew how to use it.

The military hospital admitted twenty to thirty casualties a day in early 1983. Military families are also treated there. We observed patients with a variety of battle injuries. The youthfulness of the soldiers surprised us; many were in their early teens.

The hospital staff reported major problems in dealing with the soldiers' severe disabilities and accompanying depression. Better medical care and more antibiotics could undoubtedly reduce the large number of amputations we saw.

The small rural clinic we visited was operated by a group of nuns. One nurse and one physician saw sixty to seventy-five patients a day. There was no laboratory equipment, and medications and supplies were meager.

The clinic had had to move from its previous location due to repeated raids by government forces. The clinic walls and doors showed evidence of gunfire. Stories of health workers being stopped by the police and detained for carrying a small box of medicine for the clinic were common. This pattern of intimidation makes the recruiting of staff difficult and makes patients afraid to attend the clinic.

Basic public health measures are not being carried out, even in the capital city. Garbage, with an offensive stench, lines the roadsides of San Salvador in great mounds, serving as breeding grounds for rats and flies and contaminating the supply of drinking water. Malariology teams no longer perform their functions, and the incidence of malaria has increased.

Although the Ministry of Health had formerly supplied eighty-five mobile health units to areas of the countryside under the government's military control, at the time of our visit only a handful of units were in operation. Because the medical school of the national university has been closed since June 1980, there are no medical students in their final social-service year to staff the rural clinics and health posts.

The Ministry of Health gave contradictory estimates of the number of Salvadoran physicians who have left the country but consistently maintained that their departure had only a minimal effect on health-care delivery. The ministry sought to substantiate this claim by pointing out that many doctors and nurses are unemployed. However, the doctors and nurses we spoke with believed that this unemployment was in fact due to insufficient public funding.

In July 1980 a prior public-health delegation had documented systematic repression and violence against health workers, and our delegation confirmed that this repression was still present in early 1983. Health workers said that anyone who criticizes the government risks being labeled an insurgent or a supporter of the opposition. This label, in turn, can lead to loss of one's job or even to abduction, torture, and death. Even engaging in health planning — for example, the collecting of statistics on the incidence of disease — renders health workers liable to reprisal.

As in the past, physicians and medical students and their families remain the primary targets of this violence. Recently, however, nurses have also become increasingly subject to abduction, disappearance, and assassination.

One example of this campaign of repression is the fact that eight of the eleven physicians who in 1980 helped found the National Committee for the Defense of Patients, Workers, and Health Institutions have since been disappeared, killed, or forced into exile.

Another example is the fact that since our delegation left El Salvador, three physicians who spoke with us have been picked up and detained by government forces. All they had discussed with us was the availability of medications and the number and type of patients they served. Among those detained was the twenty-eight-year-old director of medical services for Lutheran World Relief in El Salvador.

Perhaps the saddest aspect of El Salvador today is the total disruption of the family unit. Women are separated from their husbands, and many children are orphaned. This is particularly true in the refugee camps.

Moreover, Salvadoran government forces, operating alongside U.S. military advisers, are destroying crops and livestock and displacing or killing the peasants who work the land. The resulting abandonment of farms contributes to the deteriorating nutritional state of the population and the attendant rise in disease rates. We anticipate that as nutrition worsens, the children will become increasingly vulnerable to the lethal effects of even the common communicable diseases.

The Santa Tecla refugee camp is one of several refugee centers in or near San Salvador. About twelve hundred people were living at the camp at the time of our visit. Approximately five hunderd had arrived in the previous three weeks, fleeing heavy air attacks in contested areas of San Vicente province. Most had come on foot. Many children arrived without parents, having been found by others en route. The camp consisted almost exclusively of women and children, with an occasional elderly man. Most of the children are under the age of ten.

We saw none of the soy flour, corn meal, rice, powdered milk, and cooking oil that Agency for International Development officials assured us were allocated to the camps. This absence may be due to the anomalous system of distributing food aid through the military, which sometimes confiscates the food for its own uses or for sale on the black market.

There were no medical personnel in this camp, and the makeshift hut that served as an infirmary contained no medical supplies. There was no ongoing program of immunization.

The mothers in the camp were hungry, and many were desperate because of their inability to provide for their children. Some of the women could no longer remember which children were theirs. Mothers approached us as though they expected us to heal their children, some of whom had high fevers and appeared to be dying.

The children at Santa Tecla were severely ill. Indeed, one of our delegation had had more than thirty years of experience observing nutritional problems in Latin and Central America and had never seen children as sick as these, except in famine areas. Most of the children had head lice. Many had scabies, fungus infections, and impetigo. Most had the rough, hyperkeratotic skin typical of vitamin deficiency. Dental caries were severe. Clinical anemia was present, as were parasitic infections.

Most of these children exhibited the apathetic demeanor characteristic of the severely malnourished. Many children were so sensorily deprived that they reached out to touch our clothes. Babies tried to suckle dry breasts. Adolescent girls often appeared to be only eight or nine years old. The whole impression was one of despondency, loneliness, depression, and hunger.

We conducted a brief nutritional survey, examining about eighty-five infants and children. The mothers and children were eager to cooperate, as this was a diversion from the limited scope of their customary activity and, perhaps, because they viewed our efforts as potentially helpful.

We obtained data on age, height, weight, skin-fold thickness, and arm circumference, and made hurried, superficial physical examinations. The sample is doubtless biased in that some of the children were too sick to participate in the measurements.

The data demonstrate that the great majority of refugee children suffer from malnutrition. Several parameters were used. Height-for-age measurements indicate that 98 percent of these children were malnourished, according to World Health Organization's standards, and 30 percent of them severely so. Other parameters produced similar results. Comparing these findings with those from a 1978 survey performed under the auspices of the Agency for International Development, we noted that the levels of malnutrition we found were more severe.

There were no school facilities or teachers at Santa Tecla. Throughout El Salvador, and particularly in the rural areas, the primary and secondary school system is in chaos. The teachers' union has been decimated by a reign of terror, its entire leadership of twenty-three having been wiped out while preparing a petition to the legislature in 1982.

The cumulative effect of these devastating conditions at Santa Tecla, and the many refugee camps like it, is that El Salvador is producing a generation of children without family support, without education, and with nutritional deficiencies. Their physical and emotional development will surely be permanently scarred.

In closing, I would like to note that very little of the millions of dollars of humanitarian aid sent by the U.S. government is used to benefit the refugees directly. Most of it goes to relieve El Salvador's balance-of-payments problem. It is government-to-government aid, which goes directly into the Central Bank of El Salvador, where it is then used to try to keep the country solvent. For instance, if the aid is used to buy wheat, that wheat is not distributed to the population free of charge but is rather distributed through the regular commercial channels.

Demonstration Elections as Counterinsurgency

Testimony of Frank Brodhead

Activist and co-author of Demonstration Elections: U.S. Staged Elections in the Dominican Republic, Viet Nam and El Salvador.

My topic today is demonstration elections as a form of counterinsurgency. It may sound funny to describe elections as a form of counterinsurgency, but there is a sense in which it is true. The insurgents, the objects or targets of a demonstration election, are we, the citizens of the United States. Demonstration elections are an important part of the system that guarantees, or attempts to guarantee, our silence.

The recent elections in El Salvador—one in 1982 and two more in 1984—have been used by the propagandists of the Reagan administration to legitimize U.S. intervention in Central America. The official line is that we are there at the invitation of a legitimately elected government. Congress has attributed great significance to the electoral process in El Salvador, at times conditioning its aid grants on the type of elections conducted.

There is a long history of corrupt and staged elections in the world, and numbers of cases where the United States has condoned, supported, or sponsored such elections. The traditional goal of U.S. support for such elections has been to install in office a candidate favored by our government.

But the staged elections in the Dominican Republic in 1966, in Vietnam in 1967, and in El Salvador in 1982 and 1984 were something new. The goal of these elections was to legitimize in the eyes of the U.S. public U.S. intervention in other countries' affairs. These demonstration elections were the first cautious response to the Vietnam syndrome, the domestic dissent against the imperial enterprise.

I think we have to ask two questions in looking at the elections in El Salvador. The first one is, Were these genuinely Salvadoran elections or were they really designed, organized, financed, staged, and directed by a foreign power? If they were the latter, the resulting government is illegitimate and lacks the authority to invite outside intervention.

A simple way to look at this is to address the question of financing. In connection with the 1984 election, reports in *The New York Times* and the *Washington Post* indicate that the U.S. government provided 3.4 million dollars in aid explicitly for projects related to the elections, such as a computer system for voter registration. Second, 6.2 million dollars from our general aid grants to El Salvador were spent on election-related activities. Finally, the day after the election we learned that the CIA had spent at least 2.1 million dollars to influence the outcome of the elections, providing 960,000 dollars in direct subsidies to Duarte's Christian Democratic party and 437,000 dollars to the National Conciliation party, the party identified with the military. How the CIA spent the other 700,000 dollars remains unknown.

Based on these disclosures, therefore, we know that the Reagan administration spent at least 11.7 million dollars on the 1984 Salvadoran elections. But this represents only the amounts publicly disclosed, and we know there was more. We know that European sources also contributed to Duarte's election fund and that funds from right-wing foundations and individuals in the United States went to Roberto D'Aubuisson.

Moreover, in the 1982 elections, and presumably again in the 1984 elections, large amounts from the U.S. Agency for International Development went to the trade unions and other organizations sponsored by the American Institute for Free Labor Development. During the long election campaign, the employees of these organizations worked essentially as party precinct workers for Duarte.

The significance of these expenditures increases when we remember that the U.S. population is about forty-five times bigger than El Salvador's. A foreign power spending 11.7 million dollars on elections in El Salvador would be like a foreign power spending over a half a billion dollars on our elections here.

If a foreign power spent over a half billion dollars on a U.S. presidential election and succeeded in getting its candidate elected president, we would denounce that election as unfair. If that president then turned around and asked the country that sponsored him to intervene militarily in the United States to crush his domestic opposition, we would rightly reject that invitation to intervene as illegitimate.

The second question we should ask about the elections in El Salvador is, Were they genuinely free elections? In order to answer that question, we need to ask, What are the necessary conditions for free elections?

I believe that there are long-, medium-, and short-term prerequisites for free elections.

One long-term prerequisite is a free press, with print and broadcast media that publicize the views of all the parties and groups, including the opposition parties. Another long-term requirement is that people can speak freely, voice their views, associate freely, and engage in political activity, without fear of violent retribution.

Finally, the people must be able to create and participate in those intermediate institutions that stand between citizens and their governments, such as unions and professional associations, church groups, and political parties. This last factor may be the most important.

The intermediate-range requirements focus more on the period of the electoral campaign. The people must be free to register to vote and to join political parties. The parties and their candidates must be free to campaign openly and safely, with no fear of intimidation or retribution. The electoral activities of the parties and the press should educate the people about the parties' ideologies and platforms.

Finally, there are a number of short-term prerequisites, which focus on what happens on election day itself. People must be free to vote if and as they choose, or to abstain. The ballots must be secret, the count must be honest, and the candidate who wins the election should get to serve his term in office.

These are long-, medium-, and short-term determinants of free elections. Unfortunately, hardly any of these requirements were met for any of the recent Salvadoran elections.

Looking first at long-term factors, free association was not permitted. The intermediate institutions that existed, such as trade unions, teachers' associations, women's organizations, Christian base communities, and opposition political parties, were harassed, attacked, and destroyed. In addition, the press was not free. The papers were all owned by the government or by forces to the right of the government. Papers that were critical of the government from the left or that advocated significant reform were closed down by using intimidation and violence.

The intermediate-range requirements also were missing. Political parties that opposed the government from the left were not permitted to participate in the campaign or to engage in any open political activity, nor did the press report or discuss their views.

The short-term factors were absent as well. Since registration took place on election day itself at the polls, the government knew whether or not you voted. Worse yet, your worst enemy could easily find out how you voted, since they used transparent ballots and ballot boxes, and each party had observers at each polling place. (One of my favorite pictures from the Salvadoran elections—you can see it reproduced in our book [*Demonstration Elections*]—is a photo of two U.S. observers looking at a ballot box, and even though the photo is poor technically, you can see the writing on the ballots inside the box.) In an atmosphere of extensive intimidation and repression, where over thirty thousand people have died in the last five years, to abstain from voting or to vote incorrectly was to take your life in your hands.

Given the fact that hardly any of the long-, medium-, or short-term prerequisites of free elections existed in El Salvador, I conclude that the elections held there were neither Salvadoran nor free.

The second question that we have to ask is, If the elections in El Salvador were neither Salvadoran nor free, why don't Congress and the U.S. people know that? How could Congress view the elections and the resulting government as legitimate and as justifying increased U.S. economic and military aid? In the study that Professor Herman and I did for our book, we concluded that the main culprit is the U.S. so-called "free press."

When the U.S. press reported on the elections in El Salvador, it ignored the long- and medium-term factors. It concentrated on only short-term factors and still missed the most important ones.

For instance, of all the articles on the Salvadoran elections in the U.S. press, fewer than 1 percent mentioned that the opposition parties were not on the ballot. As another example, it wasn't until five months after the 1982 elections that any of the mainline U.S. media reported that Salvadorans had been legally required to vote in that election. Nor did the U.S. press point out that the ballots were not secret.

Instead, the U.S. press chose to focus on the lack of overt election-day violence and on person-in-the-street interviews. Reporters talked to the official U.S. observers. These observers were sponsored by the State Department. Many of them didn't speak Spanish. They traveled from town to town by helicopter and under armed guard. They told reporters that they didn't see anyone being harassed or prevented from voting and that it appeared to them to be a free and fair election.

Reporters also interviewed Salvadorans waiting on line to vote. These interviews were often conducted through interpreters and with government soldiers standing near by. The Salvadorans would say they were voting for peace and democracy.

In fact, most of the U.S. press accepted uncritically the way the Reagan administration framed the issues: Would the guerrillas succeed in disrupting the elections, or would the peasants brave the threat of rebel bullets and turn out to vote? According to this analysis, a peaceful election and a large turnout would mean a defeat for the guerrillas and a victory for the Salvadoran government and for the Reagan-administration policy.

The U.S. press not only misinterpreted the significance of the turnout; it also failed to report accurately its size. The Salvadoran government made the turnout appear greater than it was by opening an inadequate number of polling places—only thirteen in the capital and only one or two in most other cities. This meant the people had to wait on long lines to vote, thus creating an irresistible "photo opportunity" for the TV cameras.

Moreover, the bulk of the U.S. press accepted the Salvadoran government's statistics on voter turnout without questioning them. Ray Bonner, a *New York Times* reporter in El Salvador, questioned those statistics and shortly after that was transferred to the financial page.

In closing, I want to suggest an exercise you can try on your own in order to sensitize yourself more to how slanted the U.S. press is in its reporting. Just compare how it reports on elections in so-called "friendly" countries like El Salvador with how it reports elections in Soviet-bloc countries or socialist countries or so-called "Soviet satellites" like Nicaragua.

Last February, in commenting on the forthcoming Nicaraguan elections, Secretary of State George Shultz, one of my favorite political philosophers, said the following: "An election just as an election does not really mean anything. The important thing is that if there is to be an electoral process, it must be observed not only at the moment when the people vote, but in all the preliminary aspects that make an election really mean something."

Thus, when evaluating elections in "enemy" countries, the U.S. government and the U.S. media focus on the long- and medium-term factors and on basic preconditions for democracy—whether there is a free press and whether opposition political parties are free to criticize the government and conduct political campaigns. But these are precisely the factors that are ignored in reporting on elections in "friendly" countries. We would have a much better picture of the world if we used the same pair of glasses when we looked at different places.

In summary, the elections in El Salvador in 1982 and 1984 were not genuinely national or Salvadoran elections nor were they free. Hence they were not legitimate. Neither were the governments they put in power, nor were the invitations those governments extended to the United States to intervene.

Profile of
José Napoleón Duarte

Testimony of Tommie Sue Montgomery

Professor of Political Science at Dickinson College and author of
Revolution in El Salvador: Origin and Evolution *and numerous*
articles on the church in Central America.

The current president of El Salvador, José Napoleón Duarte, was elected in March 1984 and took office in June. Many members of the U.S. Congress see Duarte as a moderate reformer, a symbol that the country is being run by a civilian, democratic, centrist government and therefore deserves our support in its struggle against the leftist guerrillas. I want to talk with you today about Duarte and the role he has played in his country's recent history and about the role the United States is playing in El Salvador.

Duarte came to the United States to attend college at Notre Dame and then returned to join the firm his father-in-law owned. Duarte's first involvement in politics was to join a small study group in 1960. That study group began in large part as a response to the Cuban Revolution, and it led to the formation of the Christian Democratic party (PDC).

The PDC grew quickly and enjoyed considerable electoral success. Duarte, the PDC candidate for mayor of San Salvador in 1964, won that election and continued in office until 1970. The party also won other mayoral elections and by 1968 controlled almost half the seats in the national assembly.

Duarte decided not to run for office again in 1970. His ostensible reason was to return to private business, but the real motivation apparently was to prepare for the presidential election in 1972.

The Christian Democrats did not do as well in the 1970 election as they had in 1968. In order to strengthen their position in the 1972 election, they formed a coalition with the Social Democrats and the Communists and called it the National Opposition Union (UNO).

The story of the 1972 election has been told many times, and most analysts agree that had the votes been counted fairly, Duarte would have won. Instead, the military party stole the election, and Duarte was arrested, beaten, and forced into exile, where he remained until late 1979.

The UNO coalition took part in the presidential elections again in 1977, and again the military stole the election and prevented a UNO victory. Huge protest demonstrations broke out. The police opened fire on a demonstration in the capital and killed almost a hundred people.

In October 1979 a group of junior officers declared a coup and installed a junta with substantial civilian participation. When it became clear that the junta was not going to control the repressive tactics of the military, most of the civilians serving in the junta or holding cabinet posts resigned. In March 1980 the PDC split over the issue of whether to stay in the government. That month Duarte joined José Antonio Morales Erlich as the second PDC representative on the junta. In December Duarte became president of the junta in a U.S.-sponsored shake-up following the murder of four North American churchwomen. He continued in that post until the 1982 election for a constituent assembly, in which the rightist parties gained control. The assembly, under pressure from the military, elected a conservative banker, Alvaro Magana, provisional president.

Earlier this year Duarte again ran for president, this time against Roberto D'Aubuisson, and Duarte won. As I mentioned before, many in Congress think that Duarte has established civilian control over the military and will do something about the human-rights abuses that have been committed by the Salvadoran military. The reality is that the military is still in control in El Salvador, and Duarte has neither the will nor the power to control the military.

Despite the fact that the military stole the election from him in 1972 and sent him into exile, when he was finally able to take office, he described the army in his inaugural address as "the great defender of democracy."

He has never stood up to the military, and he probably never will. To illustrate that, I can tell you a story that dates back to the 1960s, when he was serving as mayor of San Salvador.

Bob Armstrong, who just spoke to you, was in El Salvador then, serving in the Peace Corps. He was working with people who lived in a slum in San Salvador. Next to the slum was a vacant lot. After organizing had been going on in the neighborhood for a while, the people decided they would like to build a community center on that lot. So they asked Bob to talk to Mayor Duarte to get permission to build the center on that land. Bob went, and Duarte gave his permission.

The people built the center, but the day after it was finished, the National Guard came in and tore it down. You can imagine the people's reaction. Bob went back to Mayor Duarte's office and said, "What happened? You gave them permission to build it." Duarte looked him straight in the eye and said, "I never gave permission to build that center."

Another indication of Duarte's unwillingness to confront and control the military is that when he orders investigations of alleged massacres or other human-rights abuses by the military, he often has the investigations conducted by the same organization that was allegedly responsible for the abuse in the first place — the military.

In fact, many of the recent alleged reforms or improvements in the human-rights atmosphere in El Salvador are really part of a public-relations offensive aimed at the U.S. Congress and the U.S. public. The Salvadoran people are not so easy to fool, because they are on the scene. It is true that the statistics for death-squad killings have improved considerably, but those death-squad statistics tell only a small part of the story.

First, the death squads are becoming more selective. Their pattern used to be to kill fifty to seventy people a week, and of those ten to twenty would be political activists. Now they kill closer to twenty a week, and twelve to eighteen are political activists. Fewer people are being killed by the death squads, but their repressive impact on political activity continues to be strong.

Another important fact to remember is that the death-squad structure has not been dismantled at all. It remains in place and could at any time resume its old level of violence. Just last week one of the better-known death squads, the Secret Anti-Communist Army, warned Salvadoran labor-union activists to behave themselves or they might wind up dead.

The protection of human rights is not a priority for the Reagan administration. The administration's goal is to support the traditional power structure in El Salvador. Did Washington complain about the lack of democracy in El Salvador in 1972 when the military stole the election from Duarte? Not a peep! In fact, when a group of progressive young army officers attempted to carry out a coup in order to honor the election results and install Duarte in office, the United States helped the military conservatives (who had stolen the election in the first place) retain control by quickly flying their candidate, Colonel Molina, back to El Salvador from Taiwan, where he was on an official visit. Again in 1977 the military stole the election, and the U.S. government again saw no need to complain about the lack of democracy.

At this point Duarte is going along with the public-relations offensive. He knows on which side his bread is buttered. But there have been times when Duarte has seen through this facade to the less pleasing reality underneath. Near the end of his term as mayor, he attended a conference of city-government officials in Mexico. At that conference he condemned U.S. policy in Central America as designed "to maintain the Ibero-American countries in a condition of direct dependence upon the international political decisions most beneficial to the U.S., both at the hemispheric and world level. Thus, the North Americans preach to us of democracy, while everywhere they support dictatorships." [Webre, Stephen. *José Napoleón Duarte and the Christian Democratic Party in Salvadoran Politics, 1960–1972.* Baton Rouge: Louisiana State University Press 1979, p. 57.]

Conclusions of Law

The actions of the Reagan administration with respect to El Salvador violate the following provisions of law:

1. The War Powers Resolution, 50 USC 1541 et seq., which provides that when the President introduces U.S. troops into actual or imminent hostilities he must (a) submit the requisite report to Congress and (b) withdraw the troops within sixty-two days unless Congress approves their presence.

2. Statutory restrictions on the distribution of economic and military aid (the Foreign Assistance act of 1961 as amended, 22 USC 2304; the International Security and Development Cooperation Act of 1981, Public Law No. 97–113, § 728; 95 Statute 1555–56), in that (a) the U.S. government has provided massive amounts of aid to a government "which engages in a consistent pattern of gross violations of internationally recognized human rights"; and (b) the U.S. government has issued fraudulent certifications alleging substantial improvements in the human-rights situation in El Salvador.

3. Its obligation under the United Nations Charter, articles 1.2, 55, and 56, to respect the right of the Salvadoran people to self-determination, by intervening so massively on the side of a government that is trying to repress the attempt of the Salvadoran people to determine its own destiny.

4. The Refugee Act of 1980, Public Law No. 96–212, 94 Statute 102, by denying political asylum to almost all Salvadoran refugees.

5. Its obligations under customary international law as evidenced by the Geneva Conventions (the Fourth Geneva Convention [civilians], articles 1, 3, and 45; Protocol Additional II, article 13), by forcibly repatriating the Salvadoran refugees.

6. The U.S. scheme of counterinsurgency and the training the United

States has provided in pursuit of that scheme inevitably lead El Salvador to violate the provisions of international law in the following list. Moreover, despite the fact that U.S. authorities have been aware of these violations, the United States has continued to fund, arm, advise, assist, and direct the Salvadoran military. For these reasons the United States is also liable as a principal, accomplice, and coconspirator in relation to the following international law violations: (a) El Salvador has violated the principles enunciated at the war-crimes trials before the Nuremberg Military Tribunals by committing war crimes and crimes against humanity in its brutal repression of popular participation and in its conduct of the war; (b) El Salvador has ignored its obligations under the principal human-rights instruments (the Universal Declaration of Human Rights; the International Covenant on Economic, Social and Cultural Rights; the International Covenant on Civil and Political Rights; and the American Convention on Human Rights) to honor the fundamental rights of its own civilian population, especially their rights to be free from torture, summary execution, and cruel, degrading, and inhuman treatment and punishment; and (c) El Salvador has violated its duties pursuant to Common Article 3 and Protocol Additional II to the Geneva Conventions by its inhumane treatment of civilian noncombatants and prisoners of war.

PHOTOS

PHOTO CAPTIONS

1   Victim of Chemical Warfare
      Photo by Comisión de Derechos Humanos de El Salvador
2   Aerial bombing, Amatitan Arriba, San Vicente, 1982
      Photo by Paolo Bosio
3   Unexploded bomb, dropped by plane
      Photo by Paolo Bosio
4   Victim of Chemical Warfare
      Photo by Comisión de Derechos Humanos de El Salvador
5   Death Squad Victims
      Photo by Comisión de Derechos Humanos de El Salvador
6   Victims of Chemical Warfare
      Photo by Comisión de Derechos Humanos de El Salvador
7   Unidentified woman found raped and shot at Lomas de San
      Francisco, San Salvador
      Photo by Comisión de Derechos Humanos de El Salvador
8   Bodies of Mario Edgardo and Pablo Cartagena, found
      July 12, 1983 at Plan del Pito
      Photo by Comisión de Derechos Humanos de El Salvador
9   Unexploded bomb
      Photo by Paolo Bosio
10   Refugees of rural aerial bombings, San Vicente
      Photo by Paolo Bosio
11   Charred bodies found on highway to Mariano, San Salvador,
      Jan. 1983
      Photo by Comisión de Derechos Humanos de El Salvador
12   Victim of Chemical Warfare
      Photo by Comisión de Derechos Humanos de El Salvador

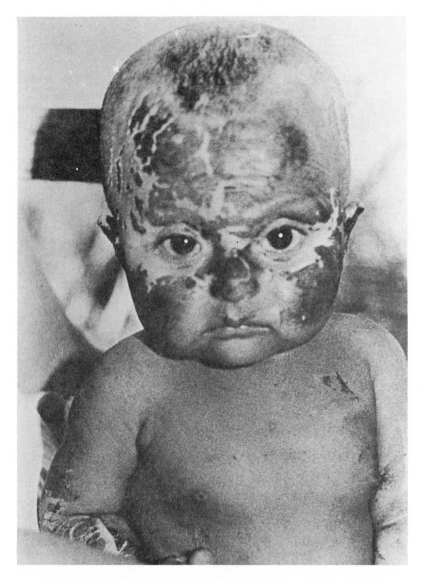

1

2

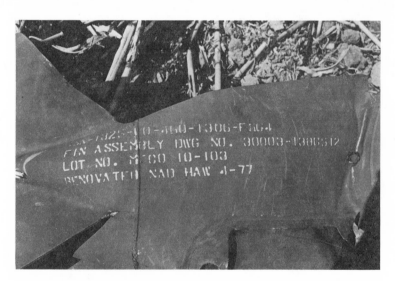

3

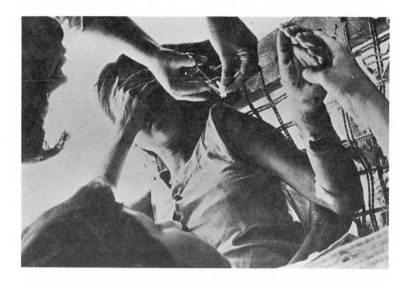

4

5

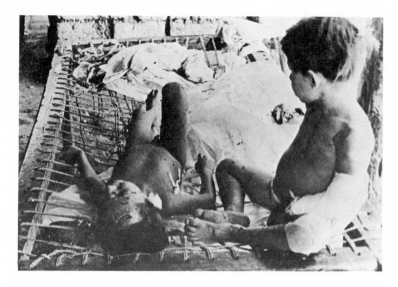

6

7

8

9

10

11

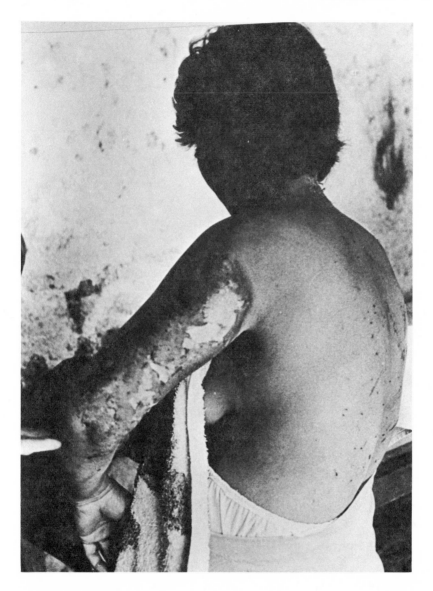

12

Guatemala

Guatemala

Findings of Fact

In the decade following the military dictatorship of Jorge Ubico (1931–44), Guatemala had two presidents who started to initiate some economic and political reforms. Because some of these reforms threatened powerful U.S. interests, the CIA sponsored an invasion from Honduras in 1954, overthrew Jacobo Arbenz, the democratically elected president, and installed a military leader.

Since 1954 Guatemala has been ruled by a series of military regimes that have more than once come to power by stealing elections. They have brutally repressed the country's civilian population. In the three decades since 1954 the Guatemalan military has killed as many as one hundred thousand Guatemalan civilians. This constitutes 1.4 percent of the population and would be comparable to three million civilian deaths in a country the size of the United States.

The Guatemalan government and military have brutally repressed all forms of popular organization and expression. Labor-union activity has been forced underground due to the many murders and disappearances of labor leaders. Priests, religious workers, academics, and members of the press have been murdered.

The repression has been particularly severe and extensive against the indigenous population in the rural areas of the country. The Guatemalan military has massacred entire villages, one of the most notorious instances being the July 1982 massacre at San Francisco Nenton, Huehuetenango, of over 350 men, women, and children.

The government's counterinsurgency program has targeted the indigenous population. The military destroys villages and forces people to move to "model villages," breaking the people's central tie to their ancestral land and forbidding such important cultural expressions as native dress, long hair, traditional crafts, and religious rites. Over seven hundred thousand peasants

53

have had to participate in civilian patrols, which are sent out on patrol inadequately armed.

Torture has been a common practice, as well as gruesome posthumous mutilation. Guatemala has become a center for counterinsurgency and genocide.

Until 1977 the U.S. role in Guatemala was quite similar to the role the United States has played in El Salvador since 1979. Between 1954 (when the CIA overthrew a democratically elected reformist regime) and 1977 (when the State Department's belated recognition of Guatemala's atrocious human-rights record led to a congressional cutoff of aid to Guatemala), the United States sent Guatemala over six hundred million dollars in economic aid and over sixty million dollars in military aid, training over three thousand troops. In the late 1960s the United States had a thousand Green Berets there, training and advising the Guatemalan military in their brutal counterinsurgency activities.

Since the Carter administration's negative human-rights report on Guatemala in 1977, overt U.S. aid has been much reduced. Congress has refused to approve any military or security assistance and has approved only modest amounts of economic and financial aid. Official aid figures, however, seriously understate the level of U.S. support to Guatemala. Military materiel already "in the pipeline" in 1977 continued to flow for years, and commercial sales of military equipment have been approved by reclassifying the equipment (for example, jeeps, trucks, helicopters) as "civilian" in nature.

The Reagan administration has been trying to restore the pre-1977 relationship of overt military aid and has been employing various strategems to evade the 1977 cutoff. Reagan has attempted to discredit international criticism of Guatemala's human-rights record and has requested a resumption of military aid. He has repeatedly flouted the congressional ban on military aid by approving the sale of military training and of spare parts and repair services for military equipment. He has supported loans to Guatemala from multilateral agencies, and he gave Guatemala ten million dollars in economic support funds (as a part of the Caribbean Basin Initiative) at a time when Congress was refusing to give Guatemala that type of security assistance.

[Editors' note: In December 1985 a civilian president, Marco Vinicio Cerezo Arévalo, was elected in the country's first relatively open elections in thirty years. Cerezo has strongly condemned the government's abuses, but it is not yet clear whether the military will cede to him the power necessary to stop them. Indeed, even on election night, hit squads were seeking out new victims.]

Oral History
by a Victim of
Government Atrocities

Testimony of Rigoberta Menchú

*Indian leader from the Province of El Quiché and a member of
the Peasant Unity Committee (CUC).*

My father died on January 31, 1980. He was participating in a demonstration, a peaceful occupation of the Spanish embassy. The Guatemalan military set the embassy on fire and killed my father and the other demonstrators by burning them alive.

My mother was captured by the government security forces and cruelly tortured. She was left tied to a tree, where she died and was eaten by dogs. We were not able to bury her body and visit her grave.

I have eight brothers and sisters, and six of them have been killed. Only three of us are left.

I tell you this because I am not special. What I have lived through is the same as what has happened to many of my people.

Guatemala is a laboratory. It is a laboratory where torture, death, and assassination are being tested out. This widespread resort to torture and murder is unprecedented in our history, and to be able to carry this out, the military needs support from outside our country.

In Guatemala the majority of the population—between 65 and 75 percent—is indigenous or Indian people. There is great linguistic diversity among the indigenous population. There are twenty-two major languages spoken in Guatemala, in addition to Spanish. I mention this because the Guatemalan government has used these differences to manipulate the Indian people.

The Indian people have a very strong attachment to the land. It is their life. It is what they live from. The people identify with their land and their village, because it is the same land and village that their families have identified with for generations.

But now the military is using violence and terror to force people to leave their traditional homes and move to fortified settlements, where the army can control their activities. This displacement is a terrible burden on the people, because it disrupts their traditional ties with their land and villages.

What has happened to these people who have been forced to leave their land? Many of them are hiding out in the mountains. I recently spent time with these people, and their living conditions are unbelievable. They have no food, and they are trying to survive by eating roots and bark and whatever they can find in the forest. They are suffering from all kinds of diseases, and they have no medical attention. Many of them are very young or very old, and many of them are dying.

Many of the displaced people have had to go to other parts of the country and are now even poorer than they were before. Many are working on plantations or land owned by agricultural export firms, where they eke out an existence, trying to earn enough to feed their families and to help them when they are suffering from diseases.

Many other Indians have seen the army take control of their communities and prevent people from organizing themselves socially and politically, or even from expressing their opinions.

Even before being uprooted and displaced by the military, the peasants of Guatemala had become very poor over the decades, because the oligarchy, the rich landowners, had gradually taken over most of the fertile land and had left only poor soil for the peasants.

Much of the best land is owned by multinational corporations like United Fruit and is used to grow food to export to rich countries. These companies exploit the land and the people, and the workers live in horrible conditions and receive very low wages. When the workers organize and demand better pay and working conditions, the government has stepped in and crushed the strikes and protected the foreign investors.

In 1954 we had a government that wanted to bring about land reform and give enough land to the peasants so they could support themselves, but the United States came in and overthrew that government. Since then the governments in our country have been uprooting the people and moving them off their land, and we have become a country of landless peasants.

Overview of Human Rights Violations by Government Forces

Testimony of Raúl Molina

Former professor and dean at the School of Engineering at the University of San Carlos, Guatemala, and rector of the university.

I want to give you a summary picture of the repression in Guatemala by citing some statistics about what has happened in my country in the last thirty years. The figures I give you are controversial; not everyone would agree with them. But many of us believe they are accurate and give a fair picture of what has been happening in my country.

First, more than one hundred thousand people have been killed by political violence and counterinsurgency activities during those three decades, and the overwhelming majority of them were killed by government forces. Since the population of Guatemala is seven million, that death toll equals 1.4 percent of the population. If 1.4 percent of the U.S. population were killed, that would be over three million people.

Second, there is the problem of those who have disappeared. In proportion to our population, more people have disappeared in Guatemala in the last thirty years than in any other country in the hemisphere—thirty-five thousand people. That's even more than the number of people who disappeared in Argentina. It's 0.5 percent of the population and would be like having over one million U.S. citizens disappear.

Third, there is the problem of the displaced. According to the Guatemalan conference of Catholic bishops, over one million people have been displaced in Guatemala, mainly because of the counterinsurgency war being waged by the Guatemalan military. Some of these people have fled the country—over one hundred thousand live in refugee camps across the border in Mexico—but most are still inside Guatemala. Some are living in fortified villages, some are struggling to survive in new areas, and some are hiding in the mountains.

Over the years the focus of the repression has shifted. While General Lucas García was president, from 1978 to 1982, the repression focused on the urban areas—on workers, professionals, and students. Under General Ríos Montt the focus shifted to the countryside, with the military engaging in a campaign of terror to relocate the peasants and control their lives. As part of this campaign the army has conducted over two hundred massacres in the rural areas, killing over ten thousand people.

Many human-rights experts, including such groups as Amnesty International and Americas Watch, agree that the human-rights situation in Guatemala is probably the worst in the hemisphere. The United Nations has repeatedly condemned these human-rights abuses and has called on the Guatemalan government to stop its campaign of relocating the rural population in order to subject it to military control.

Forms of U.S. Intervention: 1954 to the Present

Testimony of Frank LaRue

Exiled Guatemalan labor lawyer with the National Confederation of Workers and with the National Committee of Trade Union Unity.

Raúl just summarized for you the horrible conditions that my country has been living through in the past thirty years. I want to talk about why we treat those thirty years as a unit and what the role of the United States has been in my country's problems.

Guatemala's current problems started in 1954. In 1954 the CIA sponsored a coup that overthrew the government of President Arbenz. They did that because Arbenz wanted to help the poor people of Guatemala with land reform. The group that came to power in the coup was the right wing of the army, and that's the group that has ruled Guatemala ever since. Different people have served as president, but nobody who didn't follow the conservative generals' battle plan stayed in power very long. This military state is a monster that was born in 1954, was at first small and ineffective, but has since grown very powerful and sophisticated.

The United States had an important and direct role in creating this monster, first by putting the army in power in 1954 and then by arming it, training it (especially during the late 1960s), and turning it into a modern, efficient military machine. The U.S. training was so effective that the Guatemalan military can now function without U.S. military aid, and the Pentagon hopes that the armies of El Salvador and Honduras will follow Guatemala's example in this regard.

Congress cut off official military aid to Guatemala in 1977 because of Guatemala's terrible human-rights record, but now Reagan is trying to get Congress to resume military aid to Guatemala. But Congress has continued to authorize economic aid to Guatemala, and this economic aid is not used for neutral economic development. Much of it is used as part of the military's counterinsurgency program.

For instance, the economic aid is often used to build schools or roads.

59

But those schools are often built in the fortified villages where the army is relocating the peasants to control them better, and the roads allow the army to bring in its trucks and tanks and move its troops and equipment. Thus much of what is called economic development is really part of the army's campaign of counterinsurgency and population control.

Finally, it is important to point out that despite the power of the Guatemalan military, Guatemala's military government is very dependent on aid and approval from the United States and its allies, such as Israel. The Guatemalan government is sponsoring a series of elections now, and the purpose of these elections is to make the government appear legitimate and democratic. But the elections do not offer a genuine policy choice to the Guatemalan people, and the result is predetermined. Next year there will be elections for president, and we have no doubt that a civilian will be elected president, but we also have no doubt that he will ultimately be subject to military control.

Conclusions of Law

The actions of the Reagan administration with respect to Guatemala violate the following provisions of law:

1. The Foreign Assistance Act of 1961, 22 USC 2304, which forbids the provision of security assistance to governments that consistently and grossly violate human rights unless the President certifies that extraordinary circumstances exist, which Reagan has not done.

2. The International Financial Institutions Act of 1977, 22 USC 262d, which prohibits U.S. support for multilateral loans to gross human rights violators unless such assistance would serve the basic human needs of the citizens.

3. The Refugee Act of 1980, 8 USC 1101(a)(42), 1158, which provides for granting asylum to refugees with a wellfounded fear of persecution by reason of their social group.

4. Its obligations under customary international law as evidenced by Geneva Convention IV (civilians), articles 1, 3, and 45, Protocol Additional II, article 13, the Convention Relating to the Status of Refugees, and the Protocol Relating to the Status of Refugees, which prohibit forcibly repatriating refugees of civil disorder until human-rights violations in the refugees' home country cease.

5. The U.S. scheme of counterinsurgency and the training the United States has provided in pursuit of that scheme have led Guatemala to violate the provisions of international law in the list that follows. Moreover, although Congress cut off military aid to Guatemala in 1977 because of that country's notorious human-rights abuses, the Reagan administration has given Guatemala millions of dollars in security assistance, approved the sale of military services and material, downplayed its abysmal human-rights record, and repeatedly requested Congress to resume supplying military aid.

For these reasons the Reagan administration has incurred accomplice liability in relation to the following international-law violations by Guatemala:

(a) Guatemala has violated the principles enunciated at the war-crimes trials before the Nuremberg International Military Tribunals by committing war crimes and crimes against humanity in its brutal repression of popular participation and in its conduct of war.

(b) Guatemala, in its conduct of the war against its own indigenous people, is guilty of the crime of genocide as defined in the Nuremberg principles and in the Convention on the Prevention and Punishment of the Crime of Genocide.

(c) Guatemala has ignored its obligations under the American Convention on Human Rights and under customary international law (as evidenced by the Universal Declaration of Human Rights, the International Covenant on Economic, Social and Cultural Rights, and the International Covenant on Civil and Political Rights) to honor the fundamental rights of its own civilian population.

(d) Guatemala has violated its duties pursuant to customary international law (as evidenced by Protocol Additional II to the Geneva Conventions) by its inhumane treatment of civilian noncombatants and prisoners of war.

Honduras

Honduras

Findings of Fact

Honduras, which has close diplomatic and ideological ties to the United States, is the base for U.S. operations against the peoples of El Salvador and Nicaragua. This country the size of Pennsylvania now has at least eight airfields, eleven miles of tank traps near the Nicaraguan border, a radar tracking station monitoring activity in neighboring El Salvador and Nicaragua, a regional military training center, and over two thousand permanently stationed U.S. troops. This permanent presence represents the largest U.S. contingent in the region, except for the garrison at the Panama Canal. Many Hondurans believe that this military presence is undermining the civilian government and exacerbating repression of internal dissent.

Beginning in October 1981, the Reagan administration launched a series of joint military exercises in Honduras. The largest of these operations, Big Pine II, lasted for six months in 1984, with fifty-five hundred U.S. troops participating. To fund this exercise, the Department of Defense circumvented the normal appropriations process, thus bypassing the normal requirement that it seek congressional approval for such expenditures. In a report prepared by the Government Accounting Office, the comptroller general concluded that the Defense Department's use of operations and maintenance funds for training and military construction in Honduras violated federal statutes governing appropriations. These statutes essentially provide that only money specifically authorized by Congress may be used for such purposes.

The training of Hondurans at one base camp alone cost between 250,000 and 500,000 dollars. During this "training" maneuver U.S. troops built and extended three airstrips and constructed roads, tank traps, and four base camps. The U.S. military bases include housing, administration, and support facilities; runways to accommodate military planes; radar facilities; equipment; and arms. It is estimated that this illegal construction cost over 1.5 million dollars. This "temporary" infrastructure is still in use and requires a permanent contingent of U.S. troops to guard it.

Honduras shares borders with both El Salvador and Nicaragua. Many of the maneuvers in which U.S. troops participate have been specifically located on those borders. Administration officials have admitted that the purpose of the exercises is to put pressure on the Sandinista government and Salvadoran guerrillas. This admission belies the administration's assertion that these are just "normal" training maneuvers and therefore Congress need not be consulted.

Several U.S. troops have been killed or wounded in Honduras, and a helicopter carrying two members of the U.S. Senate was shot down near the Salvadoran border. U.S. troops are conducting reconnaissance flights over areas of El Salvador where U.S. "advisers" stationed on the ground have come under hostile fire. Members of the CIA have been assisting the contra rebels with forays into Nicaragua, launching flights from the airfields constructed by U.S. troops during Big Pine II. These facts demonstrate that U.S. troops, who are equipped for combat and who are involved in maneuvers near the borders in Honduras, are in situations of hostilities or imminent hostilities.

An infrastructure sufficient for waging a regional war is already in place as a result of past training maneuvers, and the Defense Department has plans for more "training." General Paul Gorman, commander-in-chief of the U.S. Southern Command in Panama during the Big Pine II operations, told a Senate committee that U.S. troops would train between twenty-five thousand and twenty-nine thousand Honduran soldiers in 1984. Moreover, Reagan-administration officials have predicted that U.S. troops would be sent to Honduras each year for the foreseeable future, envisioning a continuing U.S. presence for up to twenty more years. Considering congressional reluctance to fund such activity, the administration must continue to violate the law and circumvent congressional authority if it is to implement its plans for Honduras.

The Military Buildup
and Domestic Repression

Testimony of Leyda Barbieri

*Associate at the Washington Office on Latin America and author
of numerous articles on Honduras.*

The situation in Honduras has changed considerably in the last four
years, largely because of the Reagan administration's decision to turn that
country into a military staging and training ground, a base from which the
U.S. military can operate more effectively in Central America and from
which it can threaten and pressure the Sandinistas.

U.S. military aid has increased from under four million dollars in 1980
to over seventy-eight million dollars in 1984, and there has been considerable
U.S. military activity in Honduras that comes from other budget accounts
and is therefore above and beyond that seventy-eight million dollar amount.
The Pentagon has constructed nine airfields in Honduras, two radar stations, miles of tank traps, and storage tanks that accommodate thousands
of barrels of jet fuel.

The U.S. military has regular access to ports on each coast of Honduras
and has established a regional military training center in Honduras for
Honduran and Salvadoran officers. Moreover, the Reagan administration is
seeking additional funds to expand the facilities at the U.S. military headquarters at Palmerola, Honduras, and to install an aircraft hangar with
repair capabilities.

This extensive program of assistance, training, and construction has
been accompanied by an almost continuous series of large-scale military
operations in cooperation with Honduran and Salvadoran military units.
The Pentagon characterizes these maneuvers as training exercises, but administration spokespersons at times have conceded that one of the purposes
of these maneuvers is to intimidate and pressure the Sandinistas. The number of U.S. troops participating in these maneuvers is not public knowledge
but at times has gone as high as six thousand.

The domestic counterpart of this U.S. military buildup for the people of Honduras has been a significant increase in government repression of opposition political activity. General Gustavo Alvarez Martínez, who was chief of the armed forces during most of this period, declared war on leftist opposition groups. Government security forces resorted to arbitrary detentions, torture, and disappearances in their campaign to combat what they saw as communist tendencies in labor, peasant, church, and student organizations.

During the Alvarez period, from mid-1981 to March 1984, the Committee for the Defense of Human Rights in Honduras documented the disappearance of over one hundred persons. This figure is small compared to what has been happening in El Salvador and Guatemala, but it shows a disturbing increase in repression in Honduras, compared to the period before 1980.

The role of the government security forces in these human-rights abuses has been documented, and in some cases the police have admitted their responsibility. One notorious case is the abduction and disappearance of Inés Consuelo Morillo, who is now living in exile in Germany.

Unfortunately, those responsible for these abuses have not been punished, partly because the judicial system in Honduras is ineffective and has no jurisdiction over the security apparatus. The State Department's 1983 report on human-rights practices in Honduras argued that those responsible for abuses are disciplined, and it pointed to the example of the police chief who was responsible for the death of Juan Blas Salazar, a university student who died while being tortured by the police. It is true that after his culpability was established, the police chief was removed from his position. But he was transferred to a post in military intelligence—in reality, a promotion.

What the future holds for Honduras is unclear. General Alvarez was removed in March by other senior military officers, and there are some signs that the group that now runs the military sees that Honduran interests are sometimes quite different from U.S. interests and will be taking a more independent stance.

The U.S. desire to turn Honduras into a U.S. military base from which to enforce its will in Central America creates problems for Honduras. The United States has been training Salvadoran officers at the U.S. military training center in Honduras, and the Honduran military opposes that training, because Honduras and El Salvador have traditionally been enemies. The United States has been funding, arming, and training fifteen thousand contras on Honduran territory, and the Hondurans worry about what the contras will do in Honduras if they are decisively defeated in Nicaragua or if the United States cuts off its support.

[Editors' note: In the fall of 1985 the Hondurans began to act on their uneasiness with the growing contra presence by blocking U.S. supplies to the rebel forces. It was said that certain elements of the Honduran military wanted control over further shipments, as well as an increase in assistance to their own country in return for allowing the supplies to pass. According to U.S. and contra officials, some supplies to the contras have been channeled through El Salvador since then.]

Conclusions of Law

The actions of the Reagan administration with respect to Honduras violate the following provisions of law:

1. The War Powers Resolution, 50 USC 1541 et seq., which provides that when the President significantly increases U.S. troop strength in an area of present or imminent hostilities, he must (a) submit the requisite report to Congress and (b) withdraw the troops within sixty-two days unless Congress approves their presence.

2. The law regulating the application of appropriations, 31 USC 1301(a), and the law regulating the use of Defense Department funds for military construction, 10 USC 2802(a), 2805(b) and (c), which set limits on the extent to which the secretary of defense may lawfully expend funds for purposes for which they were not specifically approved.

Nicaragua

Nicaragua

Findings of Fact

Nicaragua is geographically the largest country in Central America and has a population of 2.8 million people.

Nicaragua had been continuously invaded and controlled by foreign governments since the sixteenth century. The Spanish ruled Nicaragua until 1821, exporting Indians as slaves and battling with the British over control of the east coast.

U.S. involvement began in the mid-1800s. For a short period William Walker, a U.S. citizen, installed himself as Nicaragua's president. By the time of the Civil War the United States had invaded Nicaragua four times.

In 1909 the United States played a major role in ousting Nicaraguan President Zelaya. U.S. Marines invaded in 1912 and maintained an almost unbroken military presence until 1933. U.S. financial advisers took over the banks and major industries, dictating Nicaraguan fiscal policies and controlling the Nicaraguan economy.

From 1927 to 1933 an army of peasants and farmers led by Augusto César Sandino waged continuous guerrilla warfare against the occupying marines and succeeded in convincing the U.S. troops to go home. But by the time the marines finally withdrew, they had created a new police force — the National Guard — and appointed Anastasio Somoza García to head it.

The first Somoza assassinated Sandino. He then staged a coup and appointed himself president. For the next forty-six years the Somoza family dynasty ruled Nicaragua. It was a reign of terror, backed by the brutal repression of the National Guard and millions of dollars in military aid from the United States.

In 1961 a group of Nicaraguans organized the Frente Sandinista de Liberación Nacional (FSLN), named after Sandino and dedicated to overthrowing Somoza and eliminating the National Guard. For eighteen years

73

the FSLN worked to unite the Nicaraguan people in the struggle against Somoza. Over fifty thousand Nicaraguans were killed during the revolution. The National Guard used napalm and aerial bombardment of all the major cities. Thousands of civilians were massacred or tortured or "disappeared." On July 19, 1979, the victorious FSLN entered Managua and was greeted by a crowd of two hundred thousand people.

A pluralistic, participatory government was formed, freeing and pardoning more than three thousand National Guardsmen to reintegrate them into society. In its first five years of existence the Sandinista government has conducted an extensive program of agrarian reform — without expropriating land from large holders who are putting their property to good use — and has succeeded in bringing about internationally recognized advances in the areas of education and public health.

Since 1979 the U.S. government has utilized first subtle, then overt measures to destabilize and overthrow the Nicaraguan government. The U.S. campaign has been waged on three principal fronts: economic measures, propaganda, and military action.

Washington's economic destabilization campaign has included the following: cancelling promised aid programs; unilaterally revoking the import quota for Nicaraguan sugar; imposing a trade embargo that includes a prohibition of the export of badly needed spare parts available only from the United States; and opposing aid and loans from international agencies.

The second prong in Washington's destabilization program is a campaign of propaganda and disinformation, aimed partly at the Nicaraguan people and partly at the U.S. public. The CIA has an immense capacity for this type of campaign: It owns outright hundreds of media companies around the world, and it has more media people on its payroll than the world's four largest news services combined.

The third prong in Washington's undeclared war against Nicaragua is military action. The U.S. government funds, trains, and directs various groups of counterrevolutionaries (or contras). The contra groups are paramilitary organizations based in Honduras and Costa Rica, Nicaragua's neighbors to the north and south. They have been conducting a campaign of terrorist violence and sabotage against the Nicaraguan people for over three years. Their goal is to overthrow the Sandinista government.

Contra training camps have operated at various times in California, Florida, Georgia, New Jersey, Texas, and Virginia, and in spite of complaints by area residents about the dangerous and illegal nature of these camps, U.S. government officials have refused to take action against them. Mercenaries and death-squad members have also been trained at military bases in the United States.

In November 1981 President Reagan approved a CIA plan to sponsor the contras. U.S. support for the contras was originally supposed to be kept a secret from the U.S. public but has since been exposed and documented and openly debated in Congress.

It is a matter of public record that the Reagan administration has spent over seventy million dollars to support the contras. [Editors' note: In 1985 Congress appropriated another twenty-seven million dollars for "nonlethal" aid to the contras. The U.S. General Accounting Office reported in early 1986 that seven million dollars of the spent funds were unaccounted for.]

There are over fifty CIA agents and other U.S. government agents in Honduras and Costa Rica assisting in the war effort. Over ninety U.S. soldiers are working with the contras and providing training and advice. U.S. personnel regularly participate in reconnaissance flights in violation of Nicaraguan airspace, and U.S. personnel were directly involved in the mining of Nicaragua's ports in February and March of 1984.

The public record, however, seriously understates the extent of U.S. government support of the contras. The Defense Department reportedly turns over material to the CIA for delivery to the contras but covers up the transfer by claiming the material is no longer valuable. The Defense Department has been conducting massive military exercises in Honduras and supplying new weapons to the Honduran military, and the Honduran military is reportedly turning over its old weaponry to the contras.

The Honduran military regularly cooperates in contra attacks and covers its retreats, and the Pentagon and the CIA reportedly encourage this cooperation.

The contras have conducted a campaign of terror against the civilian population of Nicaragua. The contras pick out teachers, health workers, and religious leaders as special targets of their terrorist attacks. Some they kidnap, torture, and rape; some they murder and mutilate. Over seventy-five hundred Nicaraguans have been killed, wounded, kidnapped or disappeared. (This casualty toll of seventy-five hundred constitutes close to 0.3 percent of the population and would be equivalent to over six hundred thousand in a country the size of the United States.)

Contra attacks on property also focus on the government's programs designed to improve public welfare. They attack schools, clinics, grain-storage facilities, and agricultural cooperatives. In addition, they attack targets important to the country's economy, such as major bridges and the fuel-storage facilities in Corinto, the country's major port.

These attacks have disrupted agricultural production and exacerbated hardship and hunger. Many families have been deprived of their homes or means of livelihood. Officially, the Reagan administration has insisted that its aid to the contras is designed to cut off the alleged flow of weapons from Nicaragua to the rebels in El Salvador. However, in spite of massive intelligence efforts, the United States has been unable to document any significant flow of weapons from Nicaragua to El Salvador in the last three years.

Moreover, the overwhelming bulk of contra activity takes place in parts of Nicaragua nowhere near the routes to El Salvador.

Administration supporters often concede that the main purpose of aiding the contras is to "Keep the pressure up" on the Sandinistas and to force them to adopt increasingly repressive and unpopular policies until they are eventually toppled.

Support of the contras is carried out without the requisite congressional assent. In 1983 Congress passed the Boland Amendment, which prohibited funding to forces that seek to overthrow the Nicaraguan government. Despite the fact that the contras have repeatedly stated that this is precisely their aim, the Reagan administration has continued to fund them.

In 1984 Congress imposed a twenty-four million dollar limit on government support for the contras. The Reagan administration has subverted the intent of this spending limit by allowing the supplementation of those public funds with massive amounts of illegal private contributions from organizations and individuals in the United States. These contributions of over ten million dollars to the contra cause, as well as the participation of private mercenary armies based in the United States, violate the Neutrality Act, and the U.S. government has a legal obligation to prosecute the contributors and the mercenaries rather than collaborate with them in violating the act.

Despite attempts by the Nicaraguan government to achieve peace, the U.S. government continues to conduct war. The Reagan administration refused to submit to the compulsory jurisdiction of the International Court of Justice in its consideration of the complaint filed by Nicaragua for the mining of its harbors.

Contadora, the organization consisting of Mexico, Panama, Venezuela, and Colombia, was supported by the U.S. government until recently, when the proposed Contadora treaty was accepted by Nicaragua. The United States does not support such a peace treaty. Instead, military escalation, plans for invasions, and economic and political sabotage are the cornerstones of U.S. policy.

[Editors' note: In February 1986, while Congress was considering a Reagan-administration request for an additional one hundred million dollars in aid to the contras, eight Latin American nations, including the Contadora countries, called for a cutoff to the contra aid and the resumption of negotiations with Nicaragua.]

History of U.S. Intervention From the Rise of Somoza I to the Fall of Somoza III

Testimony of Salvador Orochena

Nicaraguan student leader, arrested and exiled by Somoza in 1971 and graduate of Antioch Law School.

History is supposed to teach us lessons and prepare us for the future. It appears that those lessons about Nicaragua are falling on deaf ears.

Every day we hear about Nicaragua from the media: the charges by Nicaragua of imminent military intervention by the United States, Nicaragua's claim before the World Court of aggression by the United States, and Nicaragua's acceptance of the Contadora treaty and the subsequent rejection of it by the United States.

This phenomenon is not new. Throughout its history Nicaragua has been placed in direct confrontation with its sister republics in Central America. This confrontation has usually been dictated or arranged by Washington.

I will divide Nicaraguan history since independence into three main epochs. The first starts with independence and goes to the departure of the British from the Atlantic Coast of Nicaragua, which thereby ended the rivalry between England and the United States for control of the country. The second period goes from the presidency of Zelaya through the Somoza dictatorship. During this period the United States was the only imperial power influencing events in Nicaragua. The third period started in 1979, when the Sandinista revolution took power.

Central America became independent in 1821, but the political, economic, social, and religious structures did not change. The governor general appointed by Spain continued to rule, with the assistance of an advisory committee of aristocratic citizens. For a while Nicaragua became part of the Mexican empire and then part of a Central American federal republic. That federation dissolved in 1838.

Nicaragua entered a twenty-year period of chaos. Continuous quarrels between the people of Grenada and Leon prevented a stable government in the country as a whole.

In 1855 the forces of U.S. adventurer William Walker arrived. With the knowledge and consent of the U.S. government, Walker in 1856 declared himself president of Nicaragua, advocated slavery, and prepared to annex not only Nicaragua, but the rest of Central America, to the United States. Only the combined efforts of the other four republics aborted his plans.

At this time Great Britain was in full control of the Atlantic Coast of Nicaragua. In 1848 Great Britain formally notified the states of Central America that they must recognize and respect British supremacy in eastern Nicaragua. When Nicaragua protested, the answer came in the form of English war vessels, and Nicaragua was forced to accept British sovereignty over its Atlantic Coast.

At a time when the colonial powers were busy dividing the world into their respective spheres of power, England and the United States were negotiating about how to split up Nicaragua. A classic example was the Clayton-Bulwer Treaty of 1848, in which England and the United States agreed to share ownership and operation of any canal that might be built across Nicaragua.

It wasn't until 1894 that Nicaragua regained possession and control of its Atlantic Coast from Britain. This date marked the beginning of an era of almost complete monopoly over Nicaraguan affairs by the United States.

In 1894 General José Santos Zelaya became president of Nicaragua after a revolution. In 1909 counterrevolutionary forces landed in Bluefields. These forces were openly supported by President Taft, as well as by foreigners in Bluefields who opposed Zelaya because of a recent cancellation of concessions.

During the early days of the uprising, two U.S. soldiers of fortune were captured and executed by Zelaya government forces, and Washington seized on this incident as its excuse to break diplomatic relations with Managua. A note from the U.S. secretary of state to the Nicaraguan charge d'affairs in Washington expressed the attitude of the U.S. government:

> Since the Washington Conference of 1907, it is notorious that President Zelaya has kept Central America in turmoil. His regime unfortunately has been a blot upon the history of Nicaragua. The murder of the American soldiers of fortune was but the culmination of many acts of the Nicaraguan government which have rendered intercourse between the two nations impossible as long as Zelaya is in power.

The note also stated that the State Department would continue to receive both the Nicaraguan charge d'affairs and a representative of the rebel forces on an unofficial basis and that each faction would be held responsible for U.S. lives and property in their respective districts. The State Department also reserved the right to take such actions as it believed necessary to protect its interests in the "turbulent country."

Zelaya was deposed that same year. After selecting its own candidate for president of Nicaragua, the United States continued to foment rivalry between the two traditional political parties. In August 1912 the U.S. minister in Managua called upon the Nicaraguan government to protect the lives and property of U.S. citizens. The Nicaraguan minister of foreign relations responded that his government was unable to suppress the revolution by itself; he requested that the U.S. forces come to protect U.S. property and extend that "protection to all the inhabitants of the republic."

The U.S. response was formidable. The following day the marines arrived in Managua, and within two weeks there were reinforcements from the Panama Canal Zone. By November more than three thousand marines were in Nicaragua, occupying all the major cities. The occupation lasted 13 years.

In 1914 Nicaragua and the United States signed the Chamorro-Bryan Treaty. This treaty gave the United States the exclusive right, good for one hundred years, to build an interoceanic canal across Nicaragua. The United States also obtained the right to build naval bases on the Atlantic coast and in the Gulf of Fonseca. The United States paid Nicaragua three million dollars for these concessions.

The treaty was very controversial, particularly in Nicaragua and in the rest of Central America. The most serious legal challenges were protests by Costa Rica and El Salvador claiming that the treaty violated their rights.

Costa Rica maintained that the treaty violated her right to free navigation on the lower San Juan River, a right based on a treaty between Nicaragua and Costa Rica (later confirmed by President Cleveland) and on the Washington Convention of 1907. Costa Rica argued that since Nicaragua and the United States both knew of these prior agreements when they signed the Chamorro-Bryan Treaty, that treaty was illegal.

El Salvador argued that the waters of the Gulf of Fonseca were the common property of the countries bordering the gulf and not Nicaragua's private property to dispose of however she pleased. El Salvador also charged that a U.S. military presence in the gulf would threaten the autonomy of the small countries in the area.

Before the U.S. Senate ratified the Chamorro-Bryan Treaty, El Salvador and Costa Rica had made their objections known in Washington and had lodged formal protests with the Central American Court of Justice. The Senate and the State Department ignored the objections and ratified the treaty. The court upheld the protests and declared the treaty null and void, but the United States and Nicaragua ignored its ruling.

After World War I ended, a movement developed in Central America to reunite the five republics into one federation. Nicaragua's continuing adherence to the Chamorro-Bryan Treaty turned out to be the main sticking point in achieving unity. Nicaragua agreed to join the new federation, provided that all her treaties with the United States would remain in force. The other countries found these demands unacceptable. In addition to their earlier objections to the treaty, the delegates pointed out that it provided for the presence of U.S. troops in Nicaragua and denied Nicaragua the right to declare or make war without U.S. permission. The Nicaraguan delegation refused to consent to any provision designed to weaken the Chamorro-Bryan Treaty, and the dream of a united Central America remained unfulfilled.

Political quarrels resumed between the two traditional political parties, this time with Mexico intervening on behalf of the liberals. A civil war broke out, provoked by the results of a U.S. supervised election. Using the excuse of protecting U.S. lives and property, the U.S. military returned to Nicaragua in 1926. The U.S. Navy deployed fifteen warships, and over forty-five hundred marines were mobilized.

This intervention aroused unfavorable comment all over the world. Secretary of State Kellogg attributed this heavy opposition to Bolshevism. The marines remained in Nicaragua until General Sandino forced their withdrawal in January 1933.

During this second U.S. military occupation of Nicaragua the National Guard was created, and Anastasio Somoza was appointed its first director. He soon used this position to become dictator. The guard was supposed to suppress the guerrilla movement and guarantee the development of democratic institutions. In reality, the guard was a native proxy that the United States used to maintain its dominance over Nicaragua.

Extreme poverty, illiteracy, unjust land distribution, political repression, violation of basic human rights, and the insatiable greed of the dictator and his family caused many Nicaraguans to try repeatedly to change the government, but the National Guard, trained and financed by the United States, always came to Somoza's aid, preventing all attempts at rebellion by killing all rebel leaders.

The corruption and repression became so appalling that they drew worldwide condemnation of the regime and support for its overthrow. Collapse was inevitable. With the triumph of the Sandinista Revolution on July 19, 1979, Nicaragua has opened a new chapter in its history.

The striking similarities in attitude and policy between the present U.S. government and that of past U.S. administrations are not coincidental. During a news conference in July 1983 President Reagan said that it would be extremely difficult to bring about stability in the region as long as the Sandinista government remained in control of Nicaragua. These were nearly the exact words the United States used just before overthrowing the Zelaya government. The U.S. refusal to recognize the jurisdiction of the World Court with regard to Central American issues replicates the U.S. refusal to honor the decision of the Central American Court of Justice. Finally, the rejection of the Contadora Treaty, considered by many the only path to a peaceful solution in the region, is reminiscent of the aborted dream of Central American unity. Both movements foundered when Central American countries felt constrained to put their military relationships with the United States ahead of a peaceful regional arrangement. It is ironic that the arguments that El Salvador and Costa Rica made against Nicaragua back then are the same ones that Nicaragua is making now against them.

The Involvement of the CIA

Testimony of David C. MacMichael

Former analyst for the National Intelligence Council of the CIA, 1981-83.

Before I begin, I have a few introductory remarks.

As a result of my employment with the CIA, I am bound by the secrecy agreement I signed when I started working there and when I left. This agreement requires that I submit any written material or prepared testimony to the agency's publication-review board for clearance. My prepared remarks today have been submitted and cleared.

In a give-and-take interview situation I am authorized to make statements that have not previously been cleared, but I am still controlled in a number of ways. I must not mention any classified material that I have not received clearance to mention, nor may I name any persons with whom I used to work.

The decision to go forward with the covert war against Nicaragua was made while I was in the CIA. It was based on a determination that this war would interdict an alleged arms flow from Nicaragua to the Salvadoran rebels. Based on my continual review of the intelligence on this subject, I became concerned that the evidence for any such flow in the period since the early spring of 1981 was very scanty. Verifiable proof of such a flow was nonexistent. It soon became apparent to me that the true purpose of supporting the covert war was not to interdict this alleged flow of arms, but to overthrow the government of Nicaragua, the Sandinista government.

The interdiction of arms from Nicaragua to Salvadoran rebels was the sole legal justification for the decision by the Congress to support the contras. The evidence about this arms flow is as follows: From roughly November 1980 to March 1981 a number of governments in the region—including not only Nicaragua, but also Panama and Costa Rica—were involved in the transfer of arms and other supplies to the FMLN in El Salvador. Following protests and threats by the Reagan administration, this arms transfer by

Nicaragua ceased in March 1981. The administration makes public statements that this arms flow continues to exist when it knows full well that it does not.

People ask me whether I think the Reagan administration has manufactured or falsified evidence of an arms flow. I think the only significant attempt at that was in the so-called "white paper" of February 1981, which was revealed in the early summer of 1981 to be part forgery and part false analysis.

The CIA and other U.S. agencies have engaged in falsifying evidence in the past. But when they make such evidence public and subject to examination and investigation, the falsification is sometimes detected. Consequently, it is more convenient and more effective for the administration simply to lie, to claim that the arms flow exists without attempting to provide evidence.

The ultimate objective of U.S. support for the contras is to overthrow the Sandinista government. The lesser included objectives, as I heard them discussed, were to provoke the Nicaraguan government into making attacks across the border into Honduras (or possibly Costa Rica), so it could be charged with territorial aggression; to induce the Sandinista government to clamp down domestically, so it could be charged with violations of human rights; and to ruin Nicaragua's economy, thereby engendering a popular uprising, a strategy similar to the one pursued in Chile in the early 1970s.

I think U.S. policy in this regard has been an enormous failure. First, assuming for a moment that the true purpose was to interdict arms going to El Salvador, that purpose has hardly been well served. The contras have not interdicted a single shipment of arms, nor is it their expressed intention to do that. Arms continue to enter El Salvador from a variety of sources, but not from Nicaragua. Moreover, the Salvadoran insurgency is many times stronger than it was when this covert war started in 1981.

Secondly, the Nicaraguans have refused to be provoked into the sort of aggressive behavior the United States had hoped for. In fact, it recently embarrassed the U.S. government by offering to sign the Contadora draft peace treaty for Central America.

The human-rights record within Nicaragua, while not completely without flaws, has been by far the best in Central America, and the Nicaraguan government has not become repressive domestically, as had been the fond hope of the Reagan administration.

There has been a fair amount of success in the attempt to harm the Nicaraguan economy, and this has resulted in a considerable increase in what we might call the misery index in the country. However, the hoped-for economic collapse has not occurred.

It is my opinion that if the United States continues to maintain its objective of overthrowing the government in Nicaragua, it will eventually find it necessary to use U.S. armed forces in an open invasion with—in terms of loss of life alone—tremendous cost to the people of Central America and not inconsiderable cost to the people of the United States.

Administration spokespersons and editorial writers sometimes justify supporting the contras by describing our policy as one of "keeping up the pressure on the Sandinistas." I have big problems with that expression, because it sounds very sanitary and neutral, but it serves to hide something quite ugly and inhuman.

I want everyone to know and understand that in the past three years thousands of Nicaraguans have been killed in the U.S.-backed covert war. The vast majority of Nicaraguans killed have been civilians. A very large proportion of these have been women and children, and a not insignificant number have been killed in a most atrocious manner, including savage torture, summary executions, and gross mutilation.

Analogies are always tricky, but I would like you to consider that if four years ago the Ayatollah Khomeini had wanted to keep up the pressure on the United States and had done so by taking out a hostage every day and killing him, we would all probably have been appalled by the savagery and barbarity of such an act. Yet that's what this policy of "keeping up the pressure on the Sandinistas" entails: picking out three to five Nicaraguan citizens every day at random and killing them.

Is this a proper way for a great nation of 230 million people to conduct its relations with a small impoverished country of some three million souls, approximately half of whom are under the age of fifteen—all in the name of keeping up the pressure on the Sandinistas?

People sometimes ask whether it's fair to hold the U.S. government responsible for contra atrocities. I contend it is fair, and at times the State Department has come close to admitting that. Just last month, on September 1, there was a bombing raid on a Nicaraguan village called Santa Clara. The only casualties were three children. A plane involved in the bombing raid was shot down, and it turned out that the flight crew were U.S. citizens. When reporters asked how U.S. citizens could be involved in running bombing missions, a State Department spokesperson replied, "When we don't supply the money, we can't control the action."

To me, this is a very clear admission that during the period when the United States *was* providing the money for the contras—money allegedly ran out in June 1984—it was controlling the action and must bear full responsibility for the acts of its agents within Nicaragua. Thus when murders, torture, and other atrocities occur, there is no way the United States can escape responsibility by saying it can't control the actions of the men in the field.

Disregarding
the Will of Congress

Testimony of Peter Kornbluh

Research associate, Institute for Policy Studies and author, Nicaragua: The Price of Intervention.

For the past three years our government has been waging a war against Nicaragua. What I want to talk about today is the roles the President and the Congress have played in authorizing, funding, and directing that war. In particular, I want to specify several areas in which the Reagan administration has violated the laws set down by Congress and has shown cynical disregard and contempt not only for the specific legislation enacted by Congress, but also for the underlying scheme of government established by our Constitution which is that the legislature's role is to enact the laws, and the executive's role is to see that those laws are faithfully executed.

The idea of building a contra army was first brought to Congress in late 1981. William Casey, then director of the CIA, testified before the intelligence committees in both houses and secured their support by assuring them that the scope of the operation would be carefully circumscribed in a number of ways. First, the contra army would be limited in size to five hundred members, and no U.S. military personnel would be involved in the contra operations. Second, the contra operations would not be directed against economic or civilian targets in Nicaragua but would be limited to attacking the supply lines and interdicting the arms being delivered from Nicaragua to the rebels in El Salvador.

The first of these restrictions was not honored for long, and the second appears to have been ignored from the start. The number of contras trained by the CIA rose within a year from the promised five hundred to around seven thousand, an increase of 1,400 percent, and in another year rose to fifteen thousand. The contras have evidently never intercepted any significant arms shipments to the Salvadoran rebels, and the reasons for that failure are simple: For most of the period in question, no such shipments appear to have existed, and interdicting such shipments was not what the contras were trying to do in any event.

Finally, there is the question of the involvement of U.S. personnel. Here also Casey's assurances were soon ignored. I believe that a number of active-duty Green Berets have been operating with the contras in Nicaragua and so have a number of former special-forces troops and a number of CIA officers. One former Green Beret revealed that the CIA approached him in March 1982 and attempted to recruit him to "do what he did in Vietnam" — that is, fly planes from Honduras into Nicaragua and drop supplies for the contras.

As rumors and news reports filtered back, some members of Congress realized that the covert war was becoming something quite different from the limited operation Casey had originally described. In reaction, Congress tried to maintain some control over the operation by limiting its goals.

In August 1982 Congress passed a classified intelligence bill that prohibited conducting the war for the purpose of overthrowing the Sandinista government or provoking a military confrontation with Nicaragua and required that the operation be limited to interdicting arms. By December it had become apparent that the CIA was ignoring this classified legislation, so Congress sought to enact an open restriction on the covert operation.

An amendment was introduced calling for a total cutoff of funds to any group carrying out military activities in or against Nicaragua, but the majority in Congress was not yet ready for such an open break with the President. Instead, Congress passed the compromise Boland Amendment. That amendment prohibited using funds for the purpose of overthrowing the government of Nicaragua or provoking military exchanges between Nicaragua and Honduras. The amendment was a step in the right direction, but it left crucial terms undefined and failed to provide for effective enforcement.

The Reagan administration assured Congress in no uncertain terms that it was complying with the Boland Amendment. When Secretary of State George Shultz testified before a Senate committee, he had the following exchange with Senator Pat Leahy of Vermont:

> Senator Leahy: Is the Boland Amendment being followed today? It is the law of the land. Is it being followed by our country?
> Secretary Shultz: Yes, sir.
> Senator Leahy: With no reservations?
> Secretary Shultz: With no reservations.

But in fact it was clear that the Boland Amendment was being completely ignored. The principal objective of the contras remained, as it had been from the beginning, the overthrow of the Sandinista government, and the primary strategy continued to focus on attacking economic and civilian targets inside Nicaragua, targets that had no relationship to the alleged arms shipments to Salvadoran rebels.

Some administration spokespersons were willing to concede that the contras' main goal was to overthrow the Nicaraguan government, but they argued that our support of the contras was limited to their arms-interdiction activities and did not extend to their counterrevolutionary activities. Few observers believed this story to begin with, and the recent revelations about the comic-book-style manual the CIA provided the contras have destroyed its credibility altogether.

The so-called "Freedom Fighters' Manual" is a compendium of recipes for counterrevolutionary destabilization activities ranging from petty economic sabotage—like clogging toilets, putting sand in gas tanks, and calling in sick for work—to major acts of terrorism, such as burning down warehouses and police stations and assassinating Sandinista activists, or even other contras (in an attempt to create martyrs and generate sympathy for their cause). It goes without saying that these activities, which the CIA is recommending to the contras, are directed at attacking the government of Nicaragua and are very far removed from interdicting purported arms shipments to El Salvador.

The Intelligence Subcommittee of the House of Representatives investigated whether the administration was complying with the Boland Amendment and concluded that the administration had in fact been violating that law in the way it supported the contras. But in spite of this conclusion, Congress last fall again failed to cut off all funds to the contras. Instead, Congress placed a twenty-four million dollar limit or cap on the amount of funds the administration could use during fiscal year 1984 to support the contras. But just as the Reagan administration flouted the Boland Amendment in the previous fiscal year, so it has ignored the spending cap Congress imposed this year.

The Defense Department is contributing to the contras in a number of ways, and many of these contributions are not being properly accounted for as part of the twenty-four million dollar spending limit. For one thing, the Defense Department, in the course of its series of military maneuvers in Honduras, has constructed various military facilities, particularly airfields and fuel storage tanks, which are then used by contra forces or to support contra operations. There have also been significant transfers of weapons, ammunition, and supplies from the Defense Department to the contras, sometimes going directly from the Defense Department to the CIA to the contras (and valued as worthless surplus for accounting purposes), and sometimes occurring more indirectly, as when the Defense Department, in connection with the maneuvers, provides new matériel to the Honduran military, and the Honduran military in turn leaves its old matériel lying around for the contras to use.

For example, the military base and airfield constructed during joint U.S.-Honduran maneuvers at El Aguacate is now being used by the contras and U.S. personnel cooperating with them, and many of the bombing raids and supply runs into Nicaragua originate there. Similarly, the helicopter that crashed with two U.S. mercenaries aboard during the bombing raid on Santa Clara, Nicaragua, on September 1 had been transferred from the Pentagon to the CIA for contra use and had taken off from a U.S.-constructed airfield in Honduras. Every time these kinds of contributions go unreported or undervalued, the spending-limit law is being violated.

Another law that the Reagan administration has violated by its support of the contras is the Neutrality Act, which prohibits carrying out on U.S. soil any actions that go toward organizing or supporting military activities directed against countries with which we are at peace. The administration has allowed the contras to set up training camps at various times in a number of different states, and these camps have operated in violation of the Neutrality Act.

Finally, I believe the administration has also violated the War Powers Act. U.S. troops have conducted intentionally provocative maneuvers right across the border from Nicaragua, and some U.S. personnel have actually been cooperating with the contras in their activities inside Nicaragua. The fact that these troops have been exposed to hostile fire is clear from the incident last January in which a U.S. Army helicopter was shot down on the border and its pilot died. This exposure to hostile fire triggers the President's duty under the War Powers Act to submit a report to Congress and to withdraw the troops within sixty days, both of which he has failed to do.

The Arms Control and Foreign Policy Caucus, a bipartisan group of senators and representatives, recently issued a report discussing thirty laws that the Reagan administration appears to be violating in Central America. That report finds "a troubling pattern of disrespect and disregard for the law. Not only have numerous individual laws been violated, but perhaps of more concern, the American tradition of respect for the law is being challenged."

Techniques of Destabilization

Testimony of William Schaap

Coeditor of Covert Action Information Bulletin *and attorney at the Center for Constitutional Rights.*

I have been asked to speak briefly on the efforts by the U.S. administration to destabilize the government of Nicaragua. These efforts have been so massive and so intricate that in the fifteen or twenty minutes allotted I can only touch on the highlights of this campaign.

Destabilization can theoretically have as its goal the disruption of a government short of its overthrow, but this is hardly the case in Nicaragua, and it rarely is elsewhere. Even before the Reagan administration took office, it desired the overthrow of the Sandinista government. This was an objective in the Heritage Foundation's "Agenda for the Eighties," and it was adopted, as most of that document was, in the 1980 Republican platform. [Editors' Note: The Heritage Foundation is a Washington D.C.-based, right-wing think-tank.]

Since an overthrow by direct military intervention seemed, at least in the beginning, impractical or impolitic, destabilization was the chosen path. I should point out, however, that this administration has demonstrated—in its invasion of Grenada—that if years of attempts to topple a government by destabilization fail, the alternative can rapidly be adopted.

Although public actions are rarely thought of in the same context as covert operations, destabilizing actions may be covert or overt. If, for example, the United States wants to prevent a European ally from making a loan to Nicaragua, it can make a public request or a secret deal. In either case the goal of economic destabilization is the same. The difference, of course, is that when the action is covert, there is no public debate here or in the other country. In my testimony today I will concentrate on those actions for which there has been an effort to keep the U.S. role hidden.

In the case of Nicaragua, of course, there has been a remarkable deviation from the level of secrecy that usually surrounds covert operations. No covert action in history, with the possible exception of the Bay of Pigs invasion, has been so thoroughly exposed, and never before has one been so exposed while still in progress. While this may indicate the unusually high level of public opposition to the administration's machinations, it may unfortunately also indicate a deliberate attempt to inure the U.S. public to the war against Nicaragua, to blunt opposition if and when the direct involvement of U.S. troops escalates sharply.

Destabilization takes three main forms, and all three have been used against Nicaragua. They consist of economic destabilization, propaganda, and violence.

Most economic destabilization takes place relatively openly, so I will touch on that area only briefly. We know of the continuous efforts of the administration to thwart the making of international loans to Nicaragua. As recently as June Secretary of State Shultz sent an extremely offensive letter to the European Economic Community's Foreign Ministers' Conference on Central America, demanding that no loans or aid be given to the Sandinista government. The letter was publicly criticized by several of the foreign ministers and presumably ignored. There are other economic pressures of which we rarely hear. Private pressure can be put on U.S. manufacturers not to supply products or parts to Nicaragua. The State Department can advise prospective tourists not to include Nicaragua on their itinerary. This was a major tactic used against Grenada. Other specific economic actions include canceling agricultural purchase credits, suspending loans, and halting aid programs, all of which the United States did in the first year of the Reagan administration. [Editors' note: In April 1985 the United States suspended most direct trade with Nicaragua, cutting off both exports to this country and imports into Nicaragua.]

Propaganda destabilization involves the spreading of disinformation — deliberate distortions of the truth or outright lies — designed to portray the Sandinista government in a bad light. This disinformation is spread in the United States, in Nicaragua, and around the world. It is least effective in Nicaragua, of course, where people can often see for themselves that the assertions are untrue, but it is not really designed for the Nicaraguans. It is designed principally to affect the U.S. public. One of the ironies of disinformation is that although the CIA is prohibited from operating within the United States, the natural and intended result of disseminating such propaganda abroad is its widespread play here at home.

The CIA spends upwards of a half billion dollars a year on media and related operations and has more media personnel in its employ than AP, UPI, Reuters, and TASS combined. The Church Committee reported in 1976 that the CIA owned — not merely influenced or controlled, but owned outright — more than 240 media organizations, including newspapers, magazines, radio and television stations, wire, news and feature services, and the like.

There are several major propaganda lines that are being orchestrated against Nicaragua. These include, first and foremost, the allegation that Nicaragua is the source of a massive flow of weapons to the FMLN in El Salvador. More recently there has been the allegation that Nicaragua is deeply involved in the international drug traffic, along with Cuba. This accusation is particularly ironic, since the CIA itself is one of the largest drug traffickers in the world. Another disinformation line is the assertion that there is intense religious persecution in Nicaragua. Yet another is that the indigenous peoples of Nicaragua are being severely mistreated, if not exterminated.

All of these assertions are untrue. Disinformation of this kind does not need even a grain of truth in it to be effective. In fact, it thrives on the common misconception that where there is smoke, there must be fire. When Steadman Fagoth [a Miskito], bought and paid for by the CIA, gives a speech in the United States saying that ten thousand Miskitos have been brutally executed by the Sandinistas, most by being buried alive or decapitated, the U.S. media — even the responsible establishment media — will assume that he is exaggerating, perhaps even wildly exaggerating, but they will not consider the possibility that what he is saying is totally untrue, that the Sandinistas have not summarily executed even one Miskito — not a thousand, not a hundred, not one.

There are similar examples with respect to other disinformation lines. The most carefully analyzed is a 1981 presidentially commissioned white paper on El Salvador, which attempted to show that there was a massive flow of arms to the FMLN through Nicaragua. Philip Agee published a line-by-line analysis of this white paper, which demonstrated that the documents presented by the administration, including those that may have been forgeries, did not prove what the government said they proved. To this day, with all the massive resources at the command of the U.S. government, there has been no hard proof presented of this alleged flow of weapons.

Of course, such evidence can also be fabricated. During the Vietnam War, at a time when the United States was trying to show a flow of weapons from North to South Vietnam, the CIA took a small boat, filled it with Soviet- and Chinese-made weapons from its vast warehouse of such items at Fort Huachuca, Arizona, shot the boat full of holes, and called the press in to see this purported evidence. Former CIA officer Ralph McGehee describes this incident in a recent book.

On the question of religious persecution, I can give another good example. In August 1983 there was an incident in the town of Masaya in which the following occurred: A large Catholic school had been seriously divided between supporters and opponents of the government. The opponents convinced the school authorities to close the school for a day of protest, and a hundred or so anti-Sandinista students barricaded themselves in the school to make sure it stayed closed. Several hundred other students, along with large numbers of townspeople, demonstrated in the street against the closing of the school. Suddenly a barrage of rifle fire came from the school. Three demonstrators in the street were killed and six wounded. It later turned out that most of the riflemen in the school were not students or local residents, but outside provocateurs who had somehow gotten inside the school with the antigovernment students.

But what I want to tell you about is what happened in the media. A picture of the townspeople face down on the street and crawling for cover was sent from Nicaragua by the Associated Press and several other wire services. It appeared in many Central American newspapers with the caption, "Catholic Students Take Cover from Sandinista Bullets." (Associated Press insisted that it had transmitted the correct caption, but they never produced it.) Around the world there were stories that the Sandinistas had opened fire on a group of defenseless Catholic students, killing several. The story was deliberately twisted, and immense damage was done.

A related incident occurred later the same day when the correspondent for the Mexico City *Daily Excelsior* filed two stories, one on the arrest of eighty-one people inside the school and the other on five foreign priests implicated in the Masaya disturbances who had taken refuge in their countries' embassies that day. The lead story in Mexico City bore the headline, "81 Priests Arrested in Managua." One story was about eighty-one people being arrested, and the other story was about five priests taking refuge, but the story that went out across Latin America was that the Sandinistas were arresting priests by the scores.

There are hundreds of examples of such media distortions over the last few years. By and large, the establishment media are totally unwilling to investigate them, even in the face of heated denials by the Nicaraguan government.

Finally — and most important for the purposes of this tribunal — let me discuss violent destabilization, because virtually everything the United States does in this regard rises to the level of serious war crimes. I don't want to depreciate the effect of economic and propaganda destabilization. To the extent that the goal of all such activity is the increased suffering of the general population, it too has significant war-crime implications. But the violence directed against the Nicaraguan people has been massive.

The CIA is now fielding the largest private army in its history, and it is working hand in glove with the Pentagon and U.S. troops in doing so. It was apparently in November 1981 that the Reagan administration decided to wage war against Nicaragua. A secret plan, most of the details of which ultimately leaked out, was adopted to create, train, fund, and deploy a mercenary army against Nicaragua for the purpose of overthrowing its government.

For a long time these forces were trained on U.S. soil at camps in

Florida, Georgia, Texas, California, and elsewhere. Indeed, the training camps were so notorious that there were widespread complaints over the government's failure to halt the blatant violations of the Neutrality Act and of other state, federal, and international laws. It is now clear that the government was behind these camps all along, so the failure to prosecute was quite logical. There were many reports of people who appeared to be U.S. military personnel at these camps, reports that undoubtedly were true but impossible to verify.

Most of these camps have disappeared, but we have learned that the U.S. military is now training mercenaries to fight against Nicaragua right on its own bases. Mercenaries are being trained at all the special-forces bases: Fort Bragg, Fort Benning, Fort Lewis, and others. The two members of Civilian Military Assistance [a private U.S. military group] who died when their helicopter was shot down in Nicaragua last month had, in fact, received training shortly before that at Fort Bragg.

We have also learned that in addition to training mercenaries to fight like soldiers, the United States is training soldiers to fight like mercenaries. For nearly two years we have received reports of U.S. soldiers on active duty participating in contra raids from Honduras into Nicaragua.

In one typical report a radio newscaster in Washington, D.C., had met an army sergeant just returning from Central America. He told the newsman that he was a demolitions expert assigned as a platoon leader to lead five-man contra teams into Nicaragua from Honduras on missions aimed at blowing up bridges, factories, and the like.

He stated that a number of U.S. soldiers had been killed in such operations but that the bodies had been recovered and in all cases were disguised as accidental deaths inside Honduras. Indeed, several such accidental deaths have been reported in the papers. In at least one case Congresswoman Pat Schroeder from Colorado tried to investigate, but to no avail.

But the joint U.S.–contra teams get much more than manpower from the Reagan administration. They are completely financed, equipped, and supplied by the CIA and the Pentagon. In fact, as we recently learned in the aftermath of the crash of the Civilian Military Assistance helicopter, the Pentagon is turning surplus transport airplanes over to the CIA, which in turn delivers them to the contras. Most of the pilots are CIA officers or agents as well, and they have participated in bombing raids inside Nicaragua, some aimed at the Managua airport and some at the homes of high government officials.

Although the CIA game plan is to make every operation appear to be a contra action, we have learned that many of the most serious and large-scale attacks have been directly run by the CIA. These include the mining of harbors on both coasts, the fire-bombing of fuel depots—including the attack on Corinto, which necessitated the evacuation of over twenty-five thousand townspeople—and machine-gun attacks from speedboats against many port facilities.

You are receiving other testimony about the atrocities being committed by the contras. I only want to stress that their conduct is not unknown to their CIA and Pentagon controllers. We have learned that even death-squad members are being trained at our special-forces bases. The atrocities of the contras are not an unfortunate by-product of an otherwise lawful enterprise. They are part and parcel of a massive violation of the law.

Most of what I have discussed with you is not secret information. Other than the goings-on at special-forces camps, which required commissioning a person (who will remain nameless) to investigate those camps, most of the other incidents I have discussed have been reported in the U.S. media, though rarely with extended coverage or analysis and rarely with the appropriate implications drawn.

There have been, for example, many stories of U.S. soldiers dying in truck accidents in Honduras. Nobody has stopped to inquire why the rate of death from truck accidents seems to be so high on the Honduras–Nicaragua border, and nobody in the establishment media has dared to suggest that these people are dying in combat. But the information is there.

I think the conclusion of our research is that there is no independent contra war against Nicaragua. Rather, there is a CIA–Pentagon war against Nicaragua. Many of the participants in this war are contras, but many others are U.S. soldiers and CIA officers and agents, working alongside, coordinating, leading, and controlling the contras.

The Effects of the War: Economic Destruction and Human Suffering

Testimony of Father Bob Stark

Catholic priest working with the Central American Historical Institute in Managua, Nicaragua.

Before sharing with you accounts of the human costs of the U.S.-financed and CIA-directed war against Nicaragua, I'd like to place my testimony in context by giving some statistics of the overall damage that Nicaragua has suffered in the last three years because of the criminal actions of the United States.

As of May 15, 1984, there have been some 7,391 direct victims of the war. That includes 2,311 people killed, 1,900 wounded, and 3,720 disappeared or kidnapped. That death toll, considered as a proportion of the country's total population, is three times greater than the death toll the United States experienced in the Vietnam War.

In the last three years over 120,000 people have been displaced in Nicaragua due to the aggression. Proportionately, this is equivalent to 10 million persons being displaced in the United States.

This human tragedy is compounded by the incredible economic costs. The U.S. mining of Nicaragua's ports has cost Nicaragua 9 million dollars. From 1981 to 1983 there was 147 million dollars worth of damage to the economy, and in 1984 there was 128 million dollars worth of damage. These figures do not include indirect consequences.

What I would like to do now is share some personal accounts of myself and of missionaries who have had the privilege of working alongside the Nicaraguan people and who have observed the suffering they have undergone.

When I first began to work in Nicaragua three years ago, I went to work in central Zelaya, an agricultural area on the east side of Nicaragua. On March 3, 1982, after I had been there six months, I was on a mission to Companera, a small village in the mountains, when my party was surrounded and captured by the contras and held at gunpoint.

They kept us all at gunpoint until they found out that my partner and I were North American missionaries. Then they stopped pointing their guns at the two of us, but they kept them trained on the others. They picked out the community leaders, the delegates of the Word, and took them away. They killed the main leader, and they told us that they had killed him because he had been encouraging communism. They explained that what they meant by that was that he had been encouraging the people to participate in the medical-education campaigns.

This man had been an outstanding leader in our parish. He was the father of ten children. His wife was pregnant at the time and later gave birth to their eleventh child.

Despite threats by the contras, the people attended this man's funeral. When we carried the body back to the village, he was treated as a hero and martyr. The contras said they had executed him for crimes against the people—that is, supporting the medical-education campaign, which they said was communist.

Our parish included thirty-three villages and forty-three thousand people. As a result of activities by the contras, over two hundred members of the parish have died. Many of those victims were singled out for assassination because they were active in the work of the parish, and many of the rest are innocent victims of the contras' random terror. This past May, for example, the contras attacked a village when there was a big party going on and killed twenty people, including nine women and five children.

I would like to read to you from the testimony of a fellow priest, Father Jim Feltz, who has worked in this parish since 1981. It is an account of a particularly vicious attack that occurred in August and September of 1983. A task force of 350 well equipped soldiers entered the Paiwas Mountains, the area where we worked. They were accompanied by 150 civilians carrying packs, most of whom were *campesinos* who had been kidnapped in other regions. The surprise attack on Paiwas left twenty civilians dead, two women raped, and two women wounded. Eighteen homes burned to the ground, and 144 people became refugees. Here is the account by Father Feltz:

> In the township of Anito they killed six people, stole 50,000 cordobas, burned eight houses and an outboard motor boat used by the cooperative for transportation, blew up part of the chapel with a mortar shell, and, after leaving, fired another mortar shell into a group of people who had gathered to bury one of the victims.
>
> In Ocaguas the FDN "freedom fighters" murdered two campesinos. One was stabbed and had his eyes dug out before being killed; the other was hung from a beam in his own home.
>
> On the same day in Las Minitas, they burned six houses and all the clothes the cooperative had for sale. Before leaving, they killed the wife of the militia chief with a gunshot to the head.

They killed a campesino from El Quayabo who happened to be passing through Las Minitas because he was carrying a membership card from UNAG, the national association of small growers and herders.

The task force arrived in El Quayabo the next day and killed nine people. One of the victims was a 14-year-old girl who was raped by several men and later decapitated. They threw her body in a brook and placed her head in the road at the entrance to the village. They did the same with the head of another campesino.

Three women were forced to roll in the mud like pigs for the amusement of the contras. They were made to lie face down in the mud for a considerable period of time, after which the contras fired on them. One was killed, and another was wounded. Later they raped another woman.

The contras entered a house and murdered a couple in front of their three children. They burned four houses without allowing the occupants time to save their clothing or tools, just as they had done elsewhere.

The task force abducted 15 campesinos from the villages. These people were forced to join the 150 who had been kidnapped earlier in carrying packs of provisions and ammunition weighing between 80 and 100 pounds. Campesinos abducted by the contras are given one meal a day and live as prisoners, under constant threat of being shot if they attempt to escape.

However, Arcadio Pérez Méndez, a delegate of the Word in Las Minitas and the father of several militia members, did escape. He told us what his captors had said to him. "We are going to cut off your head so we can drink your blood," one of them threatened. "No," another responded. "Let's hang him until his tongue sticks out, to punish him for not telling us where his sons are."

Two women from Anito whose houses were burnt told of how the counterrevolutionaries showed them their new weapons while talking of President Reagan's support for the FDN. They also showed large sums of money. One campesino was told that he would be paid 40,000 córdobas if he joined the contras.

They stole a Bible from Valentín Velásquez, a delegate of the Word in Anito. "This way the people around here will see that we are Christians," the FDN people said.

Father Feltz concludes with a particularly poignant account from one of the young victims of the attack:

I had just spoken with Christina, the thin, fragile, ten-year-old daughter of Isabel Borge, a catechist in El Quayabo. Christina told me what had happened on September 2nd.

She was visiting two of her uncles when the contras arrived. They immediately killed her uncles, Lino and Candido, as well as a neighbor named Rosa Marín Pérez. All three were unarmed civilians.

One of the contras then decided to practice his marksmanship by using Christina as a target. Lying on the ground surrounded by other men who approached to watch the game, Christina screamed, "Don't kill me! Don't kill me!" The contras took no pity and fired four bullets into her body.

Miraculously, she survived, with superficial wounds on the top of the head and in the left hip, and deeper wounds that pierced her chest and right wrist.

That same day I spoke with Christina, the intelligence committee of the U.S. Senate had approved an extra $19 million to support covert CIA activities in Nicaragua. I remembered Christina's story and her cry of distress, her only recourse in the face of death: "Don't kill me!" In my mind her plea has been transformed into a new one: "Mr. President, don't kill us!" And that cry reverberates continuously in my mind.

I am not trying just to subject you to the gruesomeness of the war, but rather to somehow bring the voice of this suffering to this country, a suffering that is often obscured by the sanitized commercial coverage we see on television.

In a parish just to the north of us, a courageous civilian team of three women and one man work in a territory called Waslala. This is one of the areas where Somoza's National Guard imposed a particularly brutal reign of terror. Now some of the same men who used to rape, torture, and kill as officers in Somoza's National Guard are back, this time as officers in the Nicaraguan Democratic Force, and their tactics remain the same.

The Central American Historical Institute, a church-affiliated research center in Managua, has compiled the testimony of victims of contra violence in Waslala, and the following are excerpts from the institute's report:

> In an April 3rd attack on the town of Waslala, 37 civilians, 19 Nicaraguan solders, and 20 counterrevolutionaries were killed. On the same day, 25 houses were burned, more than 30 families lost all their possessions, and at least 20 people from the Waslala area were kidnapped.
>
> Three teenagers in nearby El Achote who had hid in the hills during the attack were bayonetted. One survived. An agrarian reform worker was cut into pieces, and his wife was shot — but not killed — as she watched the contras behead her 11-month-old baby.
>
> In that same attack, the contras took a campesino away from his family and tortured him, but close enough so they could hear his screams. They began by cutting his fingertips off. Then they cut his right hand off, plunged bayonets all over his body, and finally beheaded him. Their final act illustrated the holiness of their war: they carved a cross on his back.

It is this kind of bestiality that Reagan conveniently ignores when he speaks of the contras as "freedom fighters." This bestiality has not brought the Nicaraguans to their knees. On the contrary, although it has caused them incredible suffering, it has given rise to a stronger commitment and a deeper unity among the people. At least that is the case in our area in central Zelaya.

I would like to end my testimony this afternoon with a rough translation of a letter sent to the U.S. people by the mothers of the children who were killed in the attack on Santa Clara, the attack in which two U.S. mercenaries were killed.

> To the people of the United States from the mothers of Santa Clara:
> We are only a few of the mothers who have suffered the brutal aggression on the part of the U.S. We direct ourselves to you, the mothers and people in solidarity with our suffering and struggle, for we want you to know what Reagan has been making us go through.
> We have lost our daughters — still young and small — in a brutal aggression perpetrated by the genocide of the North American soldiers and the National Guard. I, Elena Rivera, lost my daughter of 12 years. Teresa Herrera lost her daughter Juana, also 12 years old. Socorro Madrina lost her beloved child of 13 years. And Maria lost her son Maximo, who was only going to help the soldiers milk the cows.
> It is very difficult to justify why Mr. Reagan is financing this brutal aggression against our people. Why should we not have the right to defend our sovereignty? We believe that every people has that right. And not only do they have that right, but their government has that responsibility. Our government is concerned about its people, and we will always support it.
> It is also difficult for us to understand what motive Mr. Reagan has in continuing the aggression against us. Mr. Reagan's mother has not suffered the death of a single one of her sons in such an inhuman way. We say "inhuman" because one should not have to lose their life for simply defending their rights. This is an inhuman aggression.
> We hope you will read these words to your people, and we hope that they reach the ears of Mr. Reagan, so that he stops this intervention against our country and our people and stops killing our children.

The letter is signed by the mothers, and then they added this note at the bottom: "We are disposed to continue to struggle for a free country. If we cannot live free, it would be better that we die free along with our daughters."

The Effects of the War: Economic Destruction and Human Suffering

Testimony of Reverend Tomás Tellez

Executive Director of the Baptist Convention of Nicaragua.

Members of the tribunal and everyone here, my name is Tomás Tellez. I am thirty-four years old, and I am from Nicaragua. My father is a Baptist minister, and I was born and raised in that atmosphere. Four years ago I began work in the health-care program of the Baptist Church in Nicaragua. I was named executive director of the Baptist Convention. This Convention has two hundred congregations throughout Nicaragua.

As a religious person, I can honestly say that it is not true that there is religious persecution in Nicaragua. We have established sixty new churches in the last five years in my country. We have eighty-eight pastors in our churches, and not a single one has complained of persecution.

The persecution we have felt in Nicaragua has been due to the Reagan administration. To date, four of our congregations have been destroyed or have disappeared due to contra attacks. We have two hundred members of our church who are now refugees due to the contra attacks. They have had to abandon the places where they lived.

Isidro Palma is the Baptist minister in the town of Bana. He was told one afternoon that later that night the population of the town would be attacked and that he and his four daughters were on a list to be kidnapped and taken to Honduras. He had no choice but to leave his community and hide. That night three hundred armed contras came and surrounded the town. They burned the cooperative and the health center and killed eight youths, including a three-month-old girl. The entire population of the town fled and now the town is abandoned.

Six hundred other villages have had to go through similar experiences in northern and southern Nicaragua.

In December 1983 Anajulia López, who was eighteen years old, was working in a health center that had been built by the Baptist Convention.

She was captured by forty armed contras. They destroyed everything in the center, stole the medicines and supplies, and then took Anajulia to the nearby river. Three days later her body was found floating in the river. She had been raped, and her head had been cut off. Her only crime was to have worked for the good of the people in Nicaragua.

Earlier this year, two members of the Evangelical Committee of Nicaragua were kidnapped, and their whereabouts are still unknown.

Many such incidents have happened just in the last month. On September 8 a religious worker and two other persons in a pickup truck were captured and disappeared. A group of contras came and fired machine guns at the moving truck. An eight-year-old boy who was in the truck was killed, and the driver and another passenger were gravely wounded but managed to survive. On September 23 fifty women were traveling on a bus to visit their sons at military school. The bus was ambushed and machine gunned. Eight of the mothers, some of them very elderly, died immediately, and nineteen were very severely wounded. On September 27 grain storage depots were attacked in a town called Pantasma and 120 hectares of corn and beans were destroyed.

We could cite innumerable examples of how the U.S.-backed contras are trying to make the lives of the Nicaraguan people impossible. The suffering and the hardships we go through are indescribable.

Our economy is in ruins because of the blockade imposed by the Reagan administration. There are no medicines in Nicaragua. There are very few raw materials for our factories. Food is in short supply. The sectors of our society that could be the most productive instead have to be involved in the fighting. Public transportation is difficult not only because we lack sufficient buses, but also because of a shortage of spare parts.

If I came here and destroyed this room that we are in, I would surely be placed in jail. If I went into your homes and killed people, I would surely be sent to the electric chair. Honorable judges and brothers and sisters, that is what the Reagan administration is doing in Nicaragua, and no one is doing anything to stop them.

We would like to appeal to the Christian values of all the people here in the United States and ask you to put an end to this so that Reagan would come to obey the law — and not only Christian laws and values, but the laws that people have set up between nations.

Why has he disobeyed what the International Court of Justice in the Hague has told him to do? Why has he violated the laws of the United States by killing people in Nicaragua and then not telling anyone here in the United States that he is doing that? We don't understand it, and that is why we ask people here in the United States that justice be done.

Lastly, I would like to tell the judges and members of the tribunal that Nicaragua is facing an imminent invasion of its territory. If this should happen, thousands of Nicaraguans will die in the first day of the invasion. The country would be destroyed in such a war. Nicaragua would become a ruined country, a vast cemetery. As Christians, we feel it is our responsibility to avoid this catastrophe.

I would like to thank the tribunal and everyone here, because I think this is a step toward justice and peace in Nicaragua. Thank you and God bless you.

Health Effects of the War: Medical Personnel and Facilities as Targets of Contra Attacks

Testimony of Richard Garfield, R.N.

Staff associate in the Division of Epidemiology of the School of Public Health, Columbia University, and former administrator for the Nicaraguan Ministry of Health.

One of the main areas in which the Sandinista government has achieved notable progress and significantly improved the lives of the people has been the area of health care. The Sandinista government has placed a high priority on increasing the availability and improving the quality of care for the poor workers and peasants. This priority is demonstrated by the fact that 12 percent of the gross national product is devoted to health care, which is one of the highest percentages in the hemisphere and double the percentage devoted to health care before the Revolution.

In the five years since the Sandinistas took power, infant mortality has been reduced over 30 percent, which is the fastest infant mortality has been reduced anywhere in the world. For further documentation of the achievements of the Sandinistas in the area of health care, I urge you to read an article published in the September 1984 issue of the *American Journal of Public Health*.

The Sandinistas' health-care programs have been one of the principal targets of the counterrevolution. So far fifty health-care facilities have had to close: forty-five small clinics, four large clinics, and one hospital. Seventeen of them were destroyed in armed attacks, and the rest were closed because the contras threatened to destroy the buildings or harm the staff.

Twenty-five employees of the Ministry of Health have been killed by the contras so far: thirteen physicians and technicians, two nurses, seven medical students, and three health educators. Of even greater import to health-care delivery, however, is the fact that at least forty volunteer health-care workers — and perhaps many more — have been killed, and many others have been intimidated.

These volunteer workers have constituted the backbone of the health-care-delivery system in the new Nicaragua. Located in small villages

103

throughout the country, they provide primary health-care services and carry out preventive programs, such as immunization and sanitation.

The contras' campaign is directed specifically at these volunteer workers. The typical pattern is that the contras will come to a village and ask who is "working for the Sandinistas," who is "an agent of the Sandinistas." They are trying to identify the people who volunteer their time to help in the government's health and education programs. Once they learn who the health workers and teachers are, they threaten to return and kill them, and they often do just that.

Thus the war has had a direct detrimental effect on the health-care situation in Nicaragua. In addition, the war has harmed the health-care situation by requiring that resources be diverted to respond to those injured by the war. A few health-care facilities have continued to operate in the areas with more intense military conflict, but these facilities must maintain a low census and stand ready to treat large numbers of war victims on short notice. Similarly, some of the larger hospitals in the country have been converted from general medical facilities to surgical centers that specialize in treating serious war injuries.

The aggression has also deterred health workers from carrying out their normal sanitation and preventive health programs in zones of conflict. Thus malaria, which had been brought under control for the first time in Central American history, is once again on the rise in areas where the contras are quite active.

The general economic situation, which is caused mainly by the war, is also adversely affecting the population's health. Malnutrition is an increasing problem, due to shortages of some foods, and the boycott and the mining have impeded delivery of medicines and medical supplies.

War-related deaths in Nicaragua already total over seven per ten thousand population. That is more than twice the death rate the United States experienced during the entire Vietnam War. One out of thirty Nicaraguans has been displaced by the war, and this incidence of internal displacement is having its predictable deleterious impact on the physical and psychological health of those involved.

CIA Manipulation of the Atlantic Coast Populations

Testimony of Judy Butler

Staff person on leave from the North American Congress on Latin America, currently working with the Nicaraguan Research and Documentation Center for the Atlantic Coast (CIDCA).

I want to talk about the situation in the region of Nicaragua known as the Atlantic Coast. Nicaraguans use the term "Atlantic Coast" to refer not just to a narrow strip of land along the Caribbean, but to the whole eastern half of the country, the section between the central mountains and the sea.

One of the main points I want you to consider is that despite very significant differences that exist between the two halves of the country, the strategy and tactics of the counterrevolution in the eastern half are strikingly similar to those in the west. If the Miskito counterrevolutionaries were autonomous indigenous forces, one would not expect them to adopt the same tactics as the rebel leaders who used to be in Somoza's National Guard. The similarity of tactics can be explained, I believe, by the fact that the Miskitos are cooperating with the ex-National Guard Officers, and both groups are being trained, advised, and directed by the U.S. CIA.

There are about 280,000 people, or 10 percent of the country's population, living in the Atlantic Coast region, which is over half the nation's territory. Over 180,000, or close to two thirds of the population, are mestizos, the same ethnic group—a Indian-European mixture—as most of the people on the Pacific Coast. Many of them are poor peasants who were pushed off their land in western Nicaragua by Somoza and other large landowners beginning in the 1950s. Of the remaining 100,000 people, about 27,000 are black Creoles, descended from a mix of Africans and Europeans. Finally, there are three distinct indigenous groups: the Miskitos, the Sumos, and the Ramas.

The largest of these three groups is the Miskito, numbering some 67,000, who live in the northeastern section of Nicaragua. Miskitos also inhabit the southeastern section of Honduras. They identify themselves more as Miskitos than as Nicaraguans or Hondurans, since their contact with those national governments has traditionally been minimal. Moreover, in 1960 the location of the border between the two countries was changed substantially, creating an artificial nationality change for Miskitos living on the northern banks of the Coco River.

Many of the differences between the two sides of Nicaragua are historical in origin. The dominant colonial power on the Pacific Coast was Spain, but the main colonial power on the Atlantic Coast, at least until the late nineteenth century, was Great Britain. The vast majority of the population in the west is Roman Catholic, but the main religion among the Miskitos is the Moravian Church, a Protestant group of German origin.

There has been fairly little U.S. investment in Nicaragua as a whole, but the majority U.S. presence was on the Atlantic Coast: growing bananas and extracting gold, silver, lumber, and fish. These activities depleted most of the area's natural resources and left the inhabitants with a standard of living significantly lower than that of the Nicaraguans living on the Pacific Coast, themselves among the poorest in Central America. The land is unproductive and swampy, and until the Revolution the region received no assistance to increase their production of subsistence crops. Many Miskito men migrated out of their villages to work for salaries in the U.S. companies.

The Atlantic Coast had traditionally been quite isolated from the rest of the country, with little communication and transportation between the two halves of the country, and few government social-service programs. During the insurrection there was not much fighting on the Atlantic Coast, and the Sandinistas knew little about the region. But since taking power, they have paid special attention to that area, because their philosophy is to help first those who need help the most.

Even before the contra war began, some Indian leaders tried to turn their people away from cooperating with government programs, to convince the people that they were harmful. For example, the government has tried to improve agricultural production among the Miskitos by encouraging the formation of cooperatives. In one village, as a result of efforts by the Agrarian Reform Institute, sixty villagers had formed three cooperatives for rice production in 1980. They had cleared new land and planted the rice. Then some men from Misurasata [an organization of Miskitos, Sumus, and Ramas formed with the Sandinistas in 1979 to work together to improve living conditions and later reformed by Brooklyn Rivera as an opposition force to the revolutionary government] came and convinced the villagers that the government's gifts of tools and credit were a "communist" trick and that later the government would take it all away. The people believed the story and abandoned the crop without even waiting for the harvest.

The counterrevolution on the east coast started in late 1981. It has consisted of paramilitary terrorist activities by contra bands made up of Miskito footsoldiers and a propaganda campaign conducted partly by infiltrators and partly via radio broadcasts from Honduras.

The leader of the bulk of this activity has been Steadman Fagoth, a charismatic Miskito leader. While he was a student in Managua in the 1970s, Fagoth worked as an informer for the Somoza dictatorship. Since 1981 he has been operating out of Honduras in an uneasy alliance with the Nicaraguan Democratic Force (FDN), the main contra group in Honduras. The alliance is uneasy because much of the CIA support for Fagoth's Miskito contras comes to him through the FDN, and Fagoth frequently complains that part of that support is siphoned off by the FDN and never reaches him. Fagoth's Miskito forces are trained by the former National Guard officers in the FDN, by Honduran military officers who are cooperating with the contras, and by U.S. personnel working with the CIA.

The goal of the counterrevolution in both halves of Nicaragua has been to alienate the Nicaraguan people from the Sandinista government. It has tried to convince people that the Sandinistas intend to impose totalitarian controls and do away with private property and religion, or even kill off ethnic minorities. And when propaganda alone is insufficient, the contras have gone after those who cooperate with the government's social welfare programs and have terrorized whole villages into leaving the country.

As in the west, the contras on the Atlantic Coast tend to avoid encounters with the Sandinista army and instead attack civilian targets. Their primary targets are individuals who have participated in such government programs as education, health care, food distribution, construction, and agricultural cooperatives. The contras single out people who are active in these programs — teachers, health-care workers, those who sell basic necessities at controlled prices — and wound, torture, rape, abduct, or kill them.

One such case that has become well known internationally is the case of Myrna Cunningham. Dr. Cunningham is a Miskito physician who, together with the nurse who was working with her, was kidnapped from a hospital by a Miskito contra band in late 1981 and taken across the border into Honduras. There the two women were repeatedly beaten and gang-raped and threatened with death. The propaganda to which Miskito contras are exposed is such that some of them believe they are doing God's work by fighting "communism". Dr. Cunningham remembers hearing Moravian hymns being sung by the Miskitos waiting for their turn to rape her. After a while the contras decided not to kill the two women, but rather to let them return to Nicaragua as a lesson to those who collaborated with the Revolution.

Another example is the case of Tom Hunter, a young Creole man who was working with some agricultural cooperatives near Pearl Lagoon. He was captured by Brooklyn Rivera's group, Misurasata, and tortured for five days before being killed. Among other things, they cut off his ears and made him eat them.

A less direct but equally tragic aspect of the contra campaign to discredit the government and build fear has been to subvert the government's health-care programs. The contras have repeatedly tried – sometimes successfully – to undermine preventive health-care projects, such as vaccinations and inoculation, by convincing the people that the pills or shots will harm them: for example, by making them sterile or turning them into communists.

Yet another important contra tactic is to pressure groups of Miskitos to leave Nicaragua for Honduras. Often, the contras scare or trick people into fleeing by telling them that the Sandinista army is about to attack them by cutting off other escape routes. It is an important recruiting tactic for the contras, who recruit new soldiers from among the refugee families. It also makes the Sandinistas look bad, because it implies that they are treating the Miskitos badly enough that they choose to flee.

In December 1983 the Sandinista government tried to promote reconciliation with the Miskitos by granting amnesty to over three hundred Miskitos who were being held in prison accused of counterrevolutionary activities. These prisoners had been held in a minimum-security open prison farm, and during their incarceration had learned to read and had acquired new job skills.

The Miskito contras were afraid that the amnesty program would constitute a propaganda victory for the Sandinistas in world public opinion and that the returning prisoners would cooperate with the revolutionary programs once back on the coast. The contras met the first threat by staging a headline-grabbing event in the international media. They surrounded the village of Francia Sirpia, destroyed the road and bridge that provided the only escape route for staying in Nicaragua, and convinced the community of twelve hundred people to go to Honduras with them. The event received a lot of international attention – in part due to a cleverly managed media campaign by Misura [a group led by Steadman Fagoth that broke away from Brooklyn Rivera's Misurasata and allied itself with the main CIA-financed contra group, the Nicaraguan Democratic Force or FDN] and in part because the Catholic bishop for the Atlantic Coast, Salvador Schlaeffer, originally from Wisconsin, accompanied the group on their trek.

To deal with the threat posed by the returned prisoners, a death-squad-style contra band came before dawn to the home of one of the amnestied prisoners, broke down the door, screamed at him that he was a spy for the government, and then machine-gunned him, his wife, and his child. Only the child survived. As you can imagine, this was very intimidating to the other pardoned prisoners.

According to one relief worker who works with Miskito refugees in Honduras, newly arrived refugees often complain about life in Nicaragua – for example about the hardships and scarcity caused by the war – but at first they do not complain that the Sandinistas committed atrocities against them. Within a few days, after Fagoth's people have had a chance to circulate, one or two spokespersons are selected, and they start telling horror stories about alleged Sandinista atrocities, the kind of stories we see occasionally in the media here.

While I'm on the topic of alleged Sandinista atrocities, let me refer to the testimony of Bernard Nietschmann, a professor of geography at the University of California at Berkeley. Professor Nietschmann testified before the Organization of American States in October 1983 that the Sandinistas had carried out what he termed widespread, arbitrary, and systematic human-rights violations against the Miskitos, including rape, torture, and summary execution, as well as systematic denial of food and other violations.

The research center I work with conducted a four-month investigation of these allegations and found them to be extremely exaggerated. We were able to document some cases of such violations, but the majority took place in the opening months of the counterrevolution, before there was an effective regional government in the area. They were neither widespread nor systematic and they in no way represented official government policy. They were rather the actions of individual Sandinista soldiers, many of whom were later punished.

One of the main tactics of the counterrevolution on both sides of the country is to attack the economy in an effort to alienate the Nicaraguan people from their government by creating scarcity and unemployment, hunger, and deprivation. In the Atlantic Coast the contras have burned down sawmills and blown up oil storage tanks that supplied energy to the mines. They have burned crops in the fields and planted mines in the roads to blow up trucks delivering food and supplies. They have reduced to ashes thousands of acres of reforestation projects, projects that the Sandinista government had provided in response, ironically, to historic demands by the Miskitos themselves.

The Reagan administration has used the Miskito situation to conduct a vicious and completely unprincipled propaganda campaign against the Sandinistas. Again and again they have lied shamelessly.

For example, Jeane Kirkpatrick appeared on the MacNeil–Lehrer program in February 1982 and accused the Sandinistas of building concentration camps for 250,000 Miskitos. The number she cited sounded dramatic but ignored the fact that there are fewer than 70,000 Miskitos in all of Nicaragua. Her characterization of the resettlement camps as concentration camps ignored the fact that living conditions for the Miskitos in the new villages is significantly better than what is available for the larger number of Nicaraguans who have been displaced by the war in the western half of the country.

Another example of the administration's lies regarding Sandinista–Miskito relations occurred in the same month in which General Alexander Haig, then secretary of state, displayed a photograph that he claimed showed Sandinistas burning the bodies of Miskitos on the Atlantic Coast. It soon turned out that the photography actually showed Red Cross workers on the Pacific Coast burning the bodies of Nicaraguans killed by Somoza's National Guard in 1978.

In his speech on May 9, 1984, Reagan accused the Sandinistas of "wiping out an entire culture," of "slaughtering thousands [of Miskitos], or herding them into concentration camps, [where] they are being starved and abused." I can assure you that not a word in that sentence is true—not a single word. Reagan knows that if the President says something often enough and acts as if he believes it, people will not question it, particularly if it is about abuse of Indians. Such abuse is too common, including by our own government, to be doubted.

What kind of revolution is it that the contras are trying to destroy? There is not time here to summarize all the various programs the Sandinista government is implementing in the areas of health, education, housing, land reform, and agricultural production. But I will try to give you a quick sense of some of the main programs and how they have been affected by the contra aggression.

In its first four years the Sandinista government doubled the number of health centers and clinics in the eastern half of the country. One fourth of those have had to close down after the contras killed, kidnapped, or intimidated health-care workers, destroyed the buildings and stole the medicines and supplies, or convinced the villagers to flee. A recent sad example of this campaign occurred this summer when the government opened a new health center in Tortuguero, and two days later the contras destroyed it.

In the southern part of Zelaya province the government succeeded in training 225 health-care workers—known as brigadistas—from 130 small communities that had previously had no health-care services. By the end of last year only 170 workers remained. The majority of those who left were scared off by the contras, and two of them were killed.

Similar statistics can be cited in other program areas. Consider the education statistics for southern Zelaya, where by the end of 1983 the number of schools and teachers had doubled and the number of students had more than tripled; one fourth of those schools have had to close because of threats and attacks by the contras.

Conclusions of Law

The actions of the Reagan administration with respect to Nicaragua violate the following provisions of law:

1. The Neutrality Act, 18 USC 960, which makes it a crime for persons in the United States to sponsor, organize, or support a hostile expedition against a foreign country with which the United States is at peace.

2. The War Powers Clause of the U.S. Constitution, article I, § 8, which forbids engaging in acts of war without the requisite congressional approval.

3. The Boland Amendment, Public Law, No. 97-377, § 793; 96 Statute, 1865 (1982), which barred the use of funds for any activities designed to overthrow the Nicaraguan government.

4. The Charter of the United Nations, article 2(4), which prohibits the threat or use of force against the territorial integrity or political independence of a country.

5. The Charter of the Organization of American States, which prohibits a state from intervening in the internal affairs of other states (articles 18 and 20) and which prohibits coercive measures of an economic or political nature (article 19).

6. Complicity in crimes against peace, crimes against humanity, and war crimes as defined by the Nuremberg Principles and the Third and Fourth Geneva Conventions of 1949, all of which prohibit gross violations of human rights, including summary execution and torture and the targeting of civilian populations.

7. The United States acted in derogation of its declaration (filed pursuant to article 36 of the Statute of the International Court of Justice) recognizing World Court jurisdiction: the United States attempted to withdraw its recognition less than a week before Nicaragua filed its lawsuit, thereby violating its agreement to give notice six months prior to withdrawing that recognition.

Grenada

Grenada

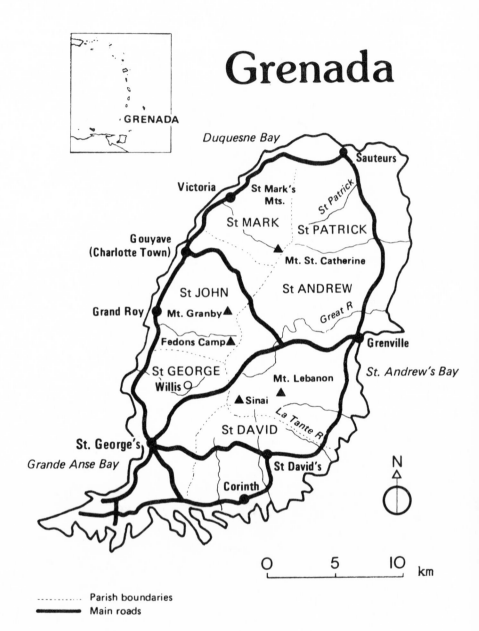

Parish boundaries
Main roads

Findings of Fact

Grenada is a tiny country, about twice the size of Staten Island, with a population of approximately 110,000. For years it was a colony, first of France, then of Great Britain. For most of the time between 1951 and 1979 it was ruled by a ruthless and corrupt dictator, Eric Gairy, who had been knighted by the British. The Grenadian people overthrew Gairy in an almost bloodless revolution, and the People's Revolutionary Government took power, led by the very popular Prime Minister Maurice Bishop.

The Carter and Reagan administrations exhibited unremitting hostility to the new government of Grenada. When Grenada asked Washington for security assistance because it feared a countercoup by the exdictator Gairy, the United States not only refused to give any aid or to extradite Gairy, but even allowed him to operate freely in Miami, recruiting Cuban exiles as a mercenary force. In addition, the Pentagon conducted military maneuvers off Puerto Rico in a thinly disguised rehearsal for invading Grenada. The National Security Council developed plans for a blockade, the CIA hatched plots for a coup, and various actual terrorist attacks appear to have had CIA backing.

Moreover, Washington discouraged tourism (vital to Grenada's economy), refused to establish normal diplomatic relations, excluded Grenada from its economic aid packages to the Caribbean area, and lobbied international agencies against granting loans and aid, including emergency food assistance, to Grenada.

An internal conflict developed within the government of Grenada in which Maurice Bishop and members of his cabinet were arrested and later killed on Wednesday, October 19, 1983.

Top U.S. officials met on Saturday, October 22, discussed plans to invade Grenada, and made a tentative decision to proceed with the invasion.

President Reagan made the final decision on Monday, October 24. That evening Reagan informed selected members of Congress of his decision, but at no time did he consult with Congress about the advisability of the invasion.

The invasion started early Tuesday morning, October 25. The press was barred from the island for over forty-eight hours.

We cannot determine the exact extent of the casualties suffered by the Grenadian people. U.S. spokespersons placed the death toll among Grenadian soldiers at one point as high as 160 but later claimed it was under 60. A Grenadian mental hospital was bombed by U.S. forces, causing the death of somewhere between seventeen and forty-seven patients. Havana reported that twenty-seven Cubans died in the invasion. In addition, hundreds of Grenadian and Cuban citizens were wounded or held prisoner for varying periods of time. Over fifty-six hundred U.S. troops took part in the invasion, of whom twenty died and over eighty-five were wounded.

The Reagan administration has offered various justifications for the invasion. These justifications are factually inaccurate and legally insufficient.

The principal justification cited early on was to rescue endangered U.S. citizens, particularly the medical students at St. George's University. In fact, those U.S. citizens were not in imminent danger. Moreover, the Reagan administration ignored signs of progress (the Grenadian government lifted the around-the-clock curfew on Monday, October 24, and four flights carrying thirty people reportedly left the island that day) and refused to respond to peaceful overtures (on Sunday, October 23, the Grenadian government offered to evacuate U.S. citizens). Finally, the U.S. military stayed in Grenada long after the so-called "rescue" had been completed.

The second principal justification was that the invasion was an exercise of collective self-defense in response to an appeal from five member states of the Organization of Eastern Caribbean States. The legal sufficiency of this justification is addressed in "Conclusions of Law" at the end of this section.

The principal underlying reason for this massive invasion and extended occupation appears to be the installation of a government more acceptable to the U.S. government.

[Editors' note: Of the 250 U.S. combat troops left in Grenada by June 1985, all but 25 Green Beret trainers were flown out. Most of a 350-man multinational peace-keeping force also left around this time. However, the U.S. troops left behind a freshly trained and organized indigenous police force of 550 officers, equipped with U.S.-provided arms, communications systems, and vehicles.]

U.S. Policy and the Invasion of October 25, 1983

Testimony of Hazel Ross

Legislative liaison for economic affairs, TransAfrica, the Black American Lobby on Africa and the Caribbean.

During the past several years the Reagan administration has repeatedly claimed that communism has secured important footholds internationally because of weak or vacillating U.S. policies. Its mission, therefore, has been to employ any means necessary to eliminate even the slightest traces of communism.

In no region of the world has this administration attempted to uphold this commitment more zealously than in the Caribbean. In this context Grenada has assumed special significance. In one fell swoop, and at little cost, the United States managed in late 1983 to stamp out communism in Grenada, to teach independent thinkers — in the Caribbean in particular — a lesson, and to restore to the U.S. psyche a sense of confidence in the United States' preeminence throughout the world.

Grenada had been viewed as an irritant to U.S. policymakers as far back as 1979. When the late Prime Minister Maurice Bishop sought U.S. security assistance in response to Eric Gairy's radio broadcasts from these shores calling for a countercoup, his request was denied by the Carter administration. Instead, Frank Ortiz, U.S. ambassador to the Eastern Caribbean states, was dispatched to warn Grenada against "develop[ing] closer ties with Cuba." Continued talk of mercenary invasions, Ortiz warned, would hurt the island's tourist industry. Then he offered Grenada the insultingly paltry sum of five thousand dollars to assist in developing the country.

When the Bishop government formalized relations with Cuba, the outraged Carter administration declared Grenada a threat to U.S. interests and began to act accordingly. A number of measures against Grenada were discussed. The National Security Council drew up a plan to blockade the country. After reviewing the options, the Carter administration rejected the blockade idea but adopted other measures designed to harass Grenada.

Under pressure from the United States, the Windward Islands Banana Association excluded Grenada from a U.S. grant to rehabilitate hurricane-damaged trees. The U.S. Agency for International Development tried to block food assistance to Grenada from the OAS Emergency Fund.

Based on advice from the State Department, some travel agents began advising clients against traveling to Grenada. In addition, a massive media campaign constantly pictured Grenada as nothing more than a Soviet or Cuban satellite.

The Reagan administration was quick to intensify the anti-Grenada sentiments engendered by the previous administration. In March of 1981 the U.S. delegate to the International Monetary Fund successfully opposed Grenada's application for 8.2 million dollars in special drawing rights to be used for capital improvements. Grenada was also refused a 3 million dollar loan from the International Development Association when the United States used its influence in the World Bank to prevent it from endorsing Grenada's public investment program.

Arguing that the proposed Grenadian international airport would accommodate Cuban military aircraft and would be used as a forward base to disrupt the U.S. supply routes to the eastern Caribbean, the Reagan administration tried to dissuade both attendance and pledges at a European Economic Community (EEC) cofinancing conference. The administration told EEC members that the airport's nine-thousand-foot runway would be larger than necessary to service tourist and commercial traffic. The fact that the airport runway in Barbados is eleven thousand feet long, in Curacao thirteen thousand, in Trinidad ten thousand, and in the Bahamas eleven thousand was considered irrelevant.

In June 1981 the United States offered four million dollars to the Caribbean Development Bank on condition that no money go to Grenada. The United States rejected Grenada's attempts to normalize relations and excluded Grenada from the benefits of the Caribbean Basin Initiative.

From August to October of 1981 the U.S. military staged maneuvers that constituted a practice run for the ultimate invasion of Grenada. On Vieques Island, the U.S. base off the coast of Puerto Rico, U.S. military personnel practiced invading "Amber" and the "Amberdines," which were code names for Grenada and the Grenadians. According to the final scenario, Amber was described as an enemy island in the eastern Caribbean where U.S. hostages needed to be rescued. After rescuing the hostages, U.S. troops would remain on the island to install a regime more acceptable to the U.S. government.

Then Secretary of State Alexander Haig rejected claims that these operations were in any way an outgrowth of U.S. hostility toward Grenada; however, the units that invaded Grenada in late 1983 were precisely the ones that had participated in the Vieques war games in 1981.

The bloody coup that left Prime Minister Maurice Bishop and many other persons dead tragically provided the Reagan administration with its opportunity for military intervention.

While stamping out communism in our own back yard, the invasion was also meant to be a clear signal to the Soviets, the Cubans, the Nicaraguans, the Syrians, and all other troublemakers.

Until the invasion of Grenada the one exception to the rule of U.S. intervention of this hemisphere had been the English-speaking Caribbean. As former colonies of Britain and as members of the British Commonwealth, these nations had not suffered the heavy-handed U.S. interventions experienced by the former colonies of France and Spain. What the Reagan administration's invasion of Grenada has done is to signal a new determination by the United States to exert control over the entire hemisphere.

The Caribbean region will long be affected by the U.S. invasion and occupation of Grenada. The key question is when and on what pretext the United States will strike again.

Prelude to the Invasion

Testimony of Joachim Mark

Grenadian historian and author of numerous articles on the Caribbean and Latin America.

On March 13, 1979, the New Jewel Movement, led by Maurice Bishop, overthrew the corrupt and repressive Gairy dictatorship and established the People's Revolutionary Government (PRG) in Grenada.

On April 8 the PRG asked the United States for security assistance against the threat of a Gairy-backed countercoup. The United States ignored this request. Instead, the U.S. Ambassador to the Eastern Caribbean, Frank Ortiz, warned Prime Minister Bishop that the United States would "view with displeasure any tendency on the part of Grenada to develop closer ties with Cuba." He suggested ominously that the PRG might soon confront "mercenary invasions by phantom enemies" and that Grenada's tourist trade would suffer. Nevertheless, Grenada and Cuba established diplomatic relations on April 14.

Ortiz's threats were not empty ones. On June 11, 1979, *Newsweek* reported that Gairy was recruiting mercenaries from among Cuban exiles in Miami, with the full knowledge of the State Department. This recruitment violated the Neutrality Act, which makes it a crime to organize paramilitary expeditions against countries with whom the United States is at peace.

Attempts by the PRG to obtain Gairy's extradition from the United States to stand trial on charges of fraud, murder, and attempted murder were ignored. Indeed, the U.S. government apparently undertook to destabilize the Grenadian government.

On November 2, 1979, a Gairy-era labor official associated with the American Institute for Free Labor Development, a CIA front, ordered the workers at the Grenada Electricity Company to shut off the power and throw the entire island into darkness. This order was part of a CIA plot to stage a coup against the Grenadian government. A police officer later convicted for his role in the plot confessed, "We were going to wait for the

American boats with mercenaries and extra arms aboard to land at three different points on the island early the next morning to make a final move."

On June 19, 1980, a bomb explosion killed three persons and injured ninety-five others at a political rally in St. George. The U.S. embassy in Barbados quickly released a statement denying U.S. involvement in the bombing.

On November 17, 1980, terrorists supported and financed by the CIA killed five Grenadians in an ambush in the parish of St. Patrick. In commenting on this incident, the Ecumenical Program for Inter-American Communication and Action (EPICA) Task Force, a research organization in Washington, D.C., stated, "The overall structure appears to be that of a single network, linked through Stanley Cyrus [a Grenadian who teaches at Howard University] to the United States."

In the diplomatic arena the United States went to great lengths to try to block assistance to the PRG from the International Monetary Fund (IMF), the World Bank, and the Caribbean Development Bank.

In part because of a glut on the world market, Grenada experienced difficulty in exporting its main crops of nutmeg, cocoa, and bananas. There was also a reduction in tourism. In his book *Grenada; the Struggle against Destabilization*, Chris Searle attributed these problems "not only to the world recession, but also in no small part to the active campaign of propaganda and destabilization orchestrated by the U.S. government."

The United States fabricated propagandistic lies about Grenada. On February 24, 1982, for example, President Reagan denounced Grenada in an address before the Organization of American States, claiming that Grenada had become a launching pad for Soviet and Cuban expansionism in the hemisphere. He warned that the island would be deprived of Caribbean Basin Initiative funds unless it adopted "principles and practices which are uniquely American." During his visit to Barbados in April 1982 President Reagan claimed that his tour of the Caribbean was intended to stop "the spread of the virus of Communism from Grenada."

Grenadian ministers and diplomats were shunned on visits to the United States and were refused the customary protocol and security measures. Dessima Williams, Grenada's ambassador to the OAS, was never formally recognized by the United States, nor did the United States accredit an ambassador to Grenada.

Meanwhile, the U.S. media launched their own propaganda offensive. Earl Bousquet, a St. Lucien journalist, complained, "There is evidence of U.S. monopoly press efforts at propaganda destabilization against the Grenada revolution."

Prime Minister Bishop was overthrown and murdered on October 19, 1983. On October 25 the United States invaded Grenada under the pretext of saving the lives of U.S. citizens who were residing there.

The invasion of Grenada had been on the drawing board for some time. Consider the following facts:

- Prime Minister Tom Adams of Barbados said in a public speech that he had been informed of plans for a U.S. intervention on October 15, which was four days before Bishop was murdered.
- Evan Galbraith, the U.S. ambassador to France, admitted in an interview on French television that the invasion "was an action which had begun two weeks ago."
- Rehearsals for the invasion began as far back as August 1981 on the island of Vieques, Puerto Rico.
- On February 27, 1983, the *Washington Post* reported that the CIA had presented to the Senate Intelligence Committee a covert action plan to destabilize and overthrow the government of Grenada.

Bill Schaap of *Covert Action Information Bulletin* has put it this way: "It is clear that in the early days of the Reagan administration it was decided to work towards the direct overthrow of the government. They had to invent an excuse that would justify an invasion, and of course it also meant that Bishop would have to be killed."

The Political and Social Effects of the Ongoing U.S. Occupation

Testimony of Margarita Samad-Matías

Director of the Latin America and Caribbean Studies Program at City College of New York and member of the first fact-finding delegation after the invasion in November 1983.

The social, economic, and political impact of the U.S. invasion of Grenada has been immense.

Grenada has a population of 110,000 people. The United States mobilized fifteen-thousand troops in the course of invading this tiny country, along with about seven hundred troops from such countries as Barbados, Antigua, and Jamaica, countries that are very dependent on and closely allied with the Reagan administration.

I would like to discuss with you today the political, economic, and social impacts of the invasion. First I will discuss the political impact, including the media and psychological aspects.

An important component of the invasion forces was the army's 350-person psychological unit, armed with advanced degrees in psychology and related fields. This unit immediately set out to discredit the People's Revolutionary Government (PRG).

One of the first places to be bombed and destroyed in the course of the invasion was the island's radio station, Radio Free Grenada. The psychological unit set up a replacement radio station, broadcasting first from boats off shore and then on the island itself. They distributed posters and T-shirts criticizing the PRG and welcoming the invaders. They detained and tortured suspected PRG activists and sympathizers and forced them to make statements renouncing future political activity.

Many Grenadian citizens died or disappeared during the invasion. The exact number has never been ascertained, nor do the forces occupying Grenada seem to want to investigate the number. It is amazing that the U.S. government has issued numbers for the U.S. casualties and the Cuban casualties—both of which have been proved false, by the way—but they have never issued figures for the total Grenadian casualties, military and civilian.

The invading forces treated prisoners inhumanely. U.S. troops kept Grenadian and Cuban prisoners cooped up individually in boxes, with small holes for ventilation and for inspection. The boxes were placed out on the airport tarmac, surrounded by barbed wire and guard dogs. The prisoners were kept in these conditions for days, through sun and rain, and were interrogated and tortured. Finally, when these abuses became widely known, the prisoners were moved to a number of smaller detention centers.

Many of these people are still in prison today, and the conditions of their confinement are in violation of internationally recognized norms. As of June 1984, eight months after the invasion, nineteen people were still being held without having been notified of the charges against them. Many prisoners who have been charged with crimes have not been able to consult with lawyers.

The United States has recently set up trials for the political prisoners, but it is naturally very difficult to hold a fair trial under a state of occupation. Most of the prisoners have seen a lawyer for no more than fifteen minutes during their year of confinement. The proceedings have been closed to the general public: They are taking place at the prison, which is off limits for most Grenadians, including prisoners' relatives and journalists.

The U.S. military occupation of Grenada has been oppressive. The occupying forces took over the beach resort hotels and replaced the attractive shrubbery with rows of barbed wire and marine guards armed with machine guns. They have shot and killed Grenadian youths.

To my knowledge, not one member of the U.S. military has been arrested for any of the various offenses they have committed against the people of Grenada, such as bombing and destroying a civilian hospital during the invasion, injuring and killing young Grenadians during the occupation, behaving offensively and aggressively in bars, forcing their way into private homes or buildings, consorting with prostitutes, and promoting illegal drugs.

The United States set up a proxy government in Grenada, which functioned under close U.S. supervision. Under this new regime many Grenadian citizens, particularly those identified with the revolutionary government, were deprived of basic civil and political rights, including the right to travel and the right to participate in political activities.

Finally, the United States is helping to sponsor new national elections in Grenada in early December in an attempt to legitimize a new, pro-United States government in Grenada. These elections will be held while the military occupation is still in place, something we normally do not view as compatible with free elections.

The most dramatic of the economic impacts of the U.S. occupation is the increased unemployment. While unemployment was reduced by the previous government from 40 to 12 percent, it has now increased to 60 percent.

In addition, many of the economic reforms of the previous government have now been reversed. The previous government had taken unused lands from large landowners and given them to peasant farmers. These lands have now been returned to the absentee landlords who hadn't been using them for years.

The U.S.-sponsored interim government has removed price controls on food items, cement, and other essentials, leading to serious inflation. Real estate prices have also been greatly affected by the invasion, increasing by 400 percent in some areas. Various economic guarantees that used to protect the Grenadian people, such as antieviction laws, have also been weakened or abolished.

The United States and its interim proxy government have also encouraged U.S. businesses to invest in Grenada. In fact, there have been recent complaints from Grenadian business people, most of whom initially supported the invasion, that their own interests are being undercut by those of U.S. businesses. On his recent visit to Grenada Secretary of State George Shultz called the island "a lucrative piece of real estate" and then proceeded to encourage U.S. business people to develop a hotel and casino industry there, as they have done on other islands.

The social impact has been just as great. First of all, many of the important social programs initiated by the People's Revolutionary Government have been discontinued. These include Radio Free Grenada, the Free West Indian newspaper, the National Women's Organization, the National Youth Organization, daycare centers, the cooperative farmers' union, agricultural centers, and many others. Textbooks and reading materials have also been removed and destroyed.

The occupation has caused the introduction of parasitical and destructive industries previously little known in Grenada, such as hard drugs (particularly cocaine) and open prostitution. Due to the occupation and the economic destruction, there has been a great increase in crime, malnutrition, eviction, and other social ills.

Immediately after the invasion the occupation forces expelled all resident aliens. This meant the separation of at least five couples. People are trying to rectify this situation in the courts, but of course it is difficult to rectify such matters in the courts when the country is in a state of military occupation.

As a result of all this, there is general social trauma, distrust, and disintegration. Families are disintegrating, socially and economically. Pressure is being put on families to evict family members who are suspected of being still supportive of the old system. People are being fired simply because they are related to people who were active in the previous government.

Finally, the medical, psychological, and emotional impacts of the invasion and the occupation have been tragic.

The People's Revolutionary Government had established a socialistic preventive health-care system that won praise throughout the world. They had doctors representing twelve medical specialties, and these doctors rotated among seven treatment facilities, so the patients would not always have to travel to the capital, as had been the case before. Now there are only two specialists, and patients must come to the general hospital in St. George on weekends. It is very difficult to see the specialists on Sundays because there is no public transportation. People wait on long lines, and they often wait two, three, or four weeks before they are seen.

We asked U.S. Agency for International Development (AID) health professionals whether they intend to reinstitute the program with the twelve specialists, and they said that a country that small does not need that many specialists. They pointed to Fort Bragg, North Carolina, which has more people than Grenada and does not have twelve specialists. The provision of medical care has deteriorated at a time when people need more care than ever.

In summary, our observations led us to conclude that the U.S. invasion and occupation of Grenada were contrary to the long-term health and social interests of the people of Grenada. Our findings reinforced our earlier position that the invasion must be condemned and that all aspects of the occupation should be immediately terminated.

Conclusions of Law

The actions of the Reagan administration with respect to Grenada violate the following provisions of law:

1. The War Powers Clause of the U.S. Constitution, article I, § 8, which grants Congress the sole power to declare war.

2. The War Powers Resolution, 50 USC 1541 et seq., which states that when the President introduces U.S. troops into hostilities, he must submit to Congress a written report detailing the circumstances requiring the intervention, its estimated scope and duration, and the constitutional or legislative authority under which he acted. Moreover, he must withdraw the troops within sixty-two days unless Congress approves their presence.

3. The Charter of the United Nations, articles 2(3), 2(4), and 33, which prohibit the use of force against the territorial integrity or political independence of any state and which require member states to settle their disputes by peaceful means.

4. The Charter of the Organization of American States, articles 3(g), 18, 20, and 21, which prohibit the use of force except in self-defense and require the peaceful settlement of disputes.

5. The Inter-American Treaty of Reciprocal Assistance (the Rio Treaty), which prohibits the use of force inconsistent with the provisions of the United Nations Charter and which requires the peaceful settlement of disputes (articles 1 and 2).

The Reagan administration argues that the invasion was a justifiable exercise of collective self-defense in response to a request from five member states of the Organization of Eastern Caribbean States (OECS). The OECS was created by treaty in 1981, largely in response to the Grenadian Revolution. The treaty does provide for collective self-defense efforts in the event of external aggression, but there are a number of reasons why that provision does not justify the U.S. invasion.

First, the treaty contemplates requests for assistance from member states, and the United States is not a party to the treaty. Second, the treaty requires a unanimous decision of the organization's eight members, but only five of them requested this intervention. Third, the treaty authorizes military action only in the event of external aggression, and there was no external aggression here until U.S. troops landed on October 25. Finally, the OECS treaty must be interpreted to conform with the OAS and United Nations charters, which prohibit armed aggression and require the peaceful resolution of disputes.

Cuba

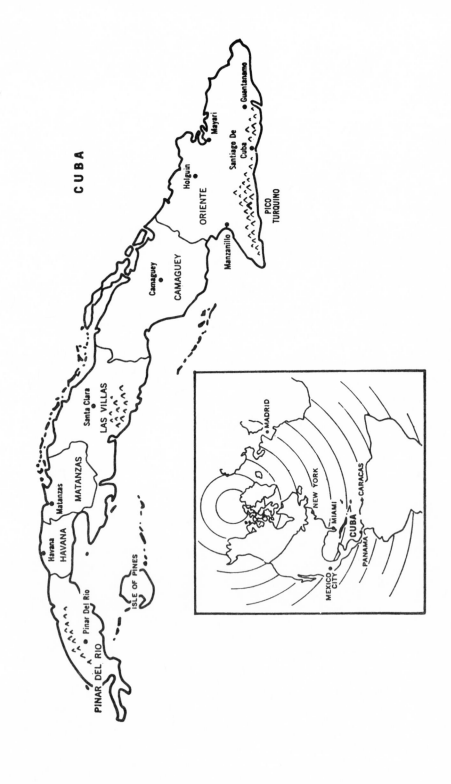

Findings of Fact

From the moment it came to power, the Cuban Revolution was perceived in Washington as a threat to U.S. hegemony in the hemisphere, because it presented a model of a sovereign and independent state pursuing national development in the service of the Cuban people. The United States has consistently used the Cuban Revolution as a justification for its opposition to popular movements in Central America and has accused Cuba of exporting revolution. Washington's reaction to this threat has been to try to force Cuba to return to its traditional subservience to U.S. interests. The campaign has had two aspects: economic pressure and covert military action.

This two-pronged attack began before Cuba nationalized any U.S. property and before Cuba established trade or diplomatic relations with the Soviet Union. In the first months of 1960 the United States began to withdraw technicians and machinery and to cut off the flow of spare parts. These were very disruptive moves, given how dependent Cuba was on U.S. technology. In March 1960 President Eisenhower ordered the CIA to begin preparing Cuban exiles for a military invasion.

The economic pressure intensified rapidly. The United States broke off trade relations with Cuba in January 1961 and imposed an economic blockade in February 1962, which it still maintains today. The blockade has cost Cuba over twenty billion dollars in lost trade, based on pre-1959 trade figures. It has disrupted the Cuban economy and caused the Cuban people great suffering.

The covert military campaign also accelerated rapidly, culminating in the disastrous Bay of Pigs invasion in April of 1961. But the CIA's paramilitary campaign against Cuba was not limited to that one invasion. Testimony at congressional committee hearings has documented the CIA role in the rebellion in the Escambray Mountains between 1962 and 1965, in over thirty other armed interventions and infiltrations, and in at least eight plots to assassinate Fidel Castro.

The CIA continues to support and use Cuban exiles, and the violent counterrevolutionary exile groups the CIA helped create continue to function. The United States still maintains its economic blockade of Cuba, and the U.S. military is increasing the number and size of its bases and garrisons throughout the Caribbean in addition to its current base in Guantanamo Bay, Cuba. Finally, the right-wing Committee of Santa Fe's May 1980 statement on U.S. foreign policy in this hemisphere, which has been adopted in large part by the Reagan administration, specifically contemplates military action against Cuba.

[Editors' note: Cuban–U.S. relations declined further in 1985, after the United States began beaming propaganda into Cuba via its new Radio Martí station. Immigration agreements between the two countries were canceled as a result. In October 1985 the United States, in addition to its previous restriction on travel by U.S. citizens to Cuba and business conducted with Cuba, severely restricted the entry of Cuban officials into the country.]

Overview: From the Bay of Pigs to Pending Threats of Invasion

Testimony of Jane Franklin

Researcher and writer associated with the Center for Cuban Studies in New York City, coeditor of Cuba Update *and author of* Cuban Foreign Relations: A Chronology, 1959–1982.

To answer the question of why Cuba became a target of U.S. aggression, we have to go back to the nineteenth century, when the United States emerged as a world capitalist power looking for foreign investment opportunities.

One of the places U.S. investors turned to was Cuba. By 1878, 83 percent of Cuba's exports were coming to the United States rather than going to Spain. Although Spain was the nominal colonial power in Cuba, the United States was becoming the actual colonial power. In the 1880s U.S. interests invested over fifty million dollars in Cuba, a huge amount of money at that time.

In 1895 José Martí led the Cuban War of Independence against Spain and would have succeeded if the United States had not stepped in. Spain was ready to grant Cuba its independence in 1898, but the United States had no intention of allowing that to happen.

Using the now familiar excuse of U.S. citizens being in danger in Havana, the United States sent in the *U.S.S. Maine*. When the *Maine* was attacked, the United States went to war with Spain, which was quickly defeated and surrendered that same year. The United States ran up its own flag. It did not even allow Cuba to come to the surrender ceremony.

In 1901 the United States agreed to withdraw its troops from Cuba if Cuba would accept the Platt Amendment, which virtually turned the country over to U.S. control. Cuba accepted the amendment in order to get the U.S. troops out. But between 1901 and 1959 there were constant revolutionary struggles in Cuba, and U.S. troops intervened whenever things seemed to be getting out of hand.

Since Cuba was a country we had traditionally controlled, it was a blow to U.S. power and prestige when the Revolution came to power on January

1, 1959. Consequently, the United States decided to destroy the Revolution and bring Cuba back into our sphere of influence. This was not just for investment purposes, but mainly because the U.S. government knew that Cuba, if it were allowed to succeed in what it intended to do, which was to feed and educate its people, would become an example to other underdeveloped countries. The Cuban leaders wanted to provide their people with healthy minds and bodies, so they could seize their own destinies and control their own lives.

In my testimony here I am going to be concentrating on events in the months following the Revolution and on why Cuba became an example that the United States is still trying to destroy.

I would like to submit into evidence the booklet I wrote, entitled *Cuban Foreign Relations: A Chronology, 1959–1982*, because it documents in detail the entire period from 1959 to 1982. From the chronology I would like to read a few items from the first year, 1959. Seizure of power was on January 1, 1959.

One of the first things the new government did was to return to a constitutional form of government. The 1940 constitution had been suspended by Batista when he took power in a coup in 1952. On February 7, 1959, Cuba adopted an amended version of the 1940 constitution as the fundamental law of the republic.

On March 3 the government took over control and management of the Cuban telephone company and immediately reduced rates. The Cuban telephone company was an affiliate of International Telephone and Telegraph, the company that later became notorious for its involvement in the overthrow of Allende in Chile.

On March 5 Ramón Grau San Martín, ex president of Cuba, demanded that the United States give up its naval base at Guantanamo. How did the United States come to have a naval base in Cuba? The United States first seized this territory by force in 1898. Then in 1901, and again in 1934, the United States pressured Cuba into leasing the base to the United States. This occupation of Cuban territory by the U.S. military became a constant source of tension between the two countries. Cuba later adopted a policy of not cashing the four-thousand-dollar yearly rental checks sent by the United States.

On March 7 Fidel Castro denounced those in the United States who were arming themselves and conspiring against the Cuban government. The Senate investigations of the CIA in 1975 disclosed that the CIA had in fact been given the go-ahead in 1959 to sponsor counterrevolutionary activity against Cuba.

On April 15 Fidel Castro came to this country on a visit. He was greeted by enthusiastic crowds wherever he went. He told the Senate Foreign Relations Committee that good relations with the United States could exist only on the basis of full equality.

He met with Vice-President Richard Nixon, who asked his opinion of dictatorship and democracy. Castro responded: "Dictatorships are a shameful blot on America. Democracy," he added, "is more than just a word. There can be no democracy where there is hunger, unemployment and injustice."

When reporters asked if the Cubans were going to export their revolution, he said no, that the revolution had come because of internal conditions. But he went on to say that Cuba's example might prove helpful to other peoples in similar situations.

On June 3 the Agrarian Reform Law went into effect, expropriating holdings larger than the new legal limit and compensating the owners. Since 75 percent of Cuba was owned by foreigners — primarily U.S. investors — this law created a furor. During the next few days there were a number of interesting developments: The Cuban consul in Miami was assaulted; the Cuban embassy in the Dominican Republic was attacked; the automobile of the Cuban ambassador to Haiti was machine-gunned; and Senator George Smathers proposed an amendment to reduce Cuba's sugar quota. The United States formally protested the new law, in particular the terms of compensation.

On June 25 Rafael del Pino, an anti-Castro leader operating from the United States as part of the anti-Castro White Rose organization, was shot down in his plane near Havana. Del Pino's activities were part of a wave of attacks against Cuba by exiles and mercenaries based in the United States.

In addition to military destabilization, the United States also tried to isolate Cuba diplomatically. On August 12 the Foreign Ministers Conference of the Organization of American States (OAS) convened in Santiago de Chile to consider such U.S.-proposed topics as "Tensions in the Caribbean" and "Effective Exercise of Representative Democracy." Cuba claimed this meeting was an obvious attempt by the United States to prejudice the OAS against the Cuban government.

On August 13 a plane from the Dominican Republic carrying arms and ten counterrevolutionaries was attacked when it landed in Cuba. The pilot turned out to be Batista's former pilot. Two invaders were killed, and the eight who were captured admitted links to President Rafael Trujillo of the Dominican Republic. (Batista at that point was still in the Dominican Republic. Later he went to Miami.)

Throughout the month of October there were frequent attacks from airplanes flying from the United States. Several attacks were aimed at sugar mills, the mainstay of the Cuban economy. Despite a formal protest by Cuba, such attacks continued. For instance, on October 21 an airplane machine-gunned Havana, killing two and wounding fifty. The next day a trainful of passengers in Las Villas Province was machine-gunned from the air.

That was the first year. But these kinds of attacks continued in succeeding years, and they haven't stopped yet. For example, in mid-1981 there was an outbreak of dengue fever in Cuba. Cuba accused the CIA of being responsible. Those who find this accusation of CIA-sponsored germ warfare farfetched or paranoid should know this: In his recent trial here in New York Eduardo Arocena, a leader in the CIA-backed anti-Castro group known as Omega 7, testified that he did in fact take germs to Cuba in 1980.

Despite all of these attempts at destabilization by the United States, Cuba has achieved some of its revolutionary goals and has greatly improved the lives of its people.

One is the tremendous health system, which was started while they were still fighting, even before they seized power. They have now developed a health system that competes with those of developed capitalist countries, as we can see by comparing the statistics. In 1970, just eleven years after the revolution, Cuban life expectancy at birth was comparable to that of the United States. With regard to infant mortality, there was a rapid decline in deaths during the first year after birth.

The second major achievement of the revolution was in the area of education. Early in the revolution Cuba waged a literacy campaign that succeeded in virtually wiping out illiteracy in the country. This campaign became a model for other Third World countries, such as Nicaragua.

Cuba's third accomplishment has been its success in preserving its revolutionary internationalism, its solidarity with other peoples engaged in similar struggles, its belief that other people have the right to determine their own destinies. Thousands of Cubans are now working in various countries around the world, helping those countries develop. In 1979 Cuba had more than two thousand health professionals working in twenty countries. Besides health workers, Cuba also sends teachers, fishery experts, and construction workers to other countries to assist in their development. As part of this solidarity with other peoples in struggle, Cuba also sends its troops when their help is requested. Cuban troops are helping the government of Angola defend itself against invasions by South Africa and against paramilitary activities by guerrilla groups supported by South Africa, the United States, and the People's Republic of China. Cuban troops are also helping Ethiopia defend itself against the invasion being conducted with U.S. support by Somalia.

In closing, I want to read something that illustrates why the United States is so threatened by Cuba, a country that has managed to achieve its goals despite U.S. efforts at destabilization. This message was sent to Fidel Castro by the general command of the Farabundo Martí National Liberation Front in El Salvador last December, on the occasion of the twenty-fifth anniversary of the Cuban Revolution:

> We would like to extend greetings through you to the people of Cuba on the occasion of the 25th anniversary of the triumph of the revolution, which is the most important and influential event in Latin American history.
>
> We extend greetings to the Communist Party of Cuba, the revolutionary government, and the revolutionary armed forces, and we greet you, our brother, who serves as a model for all Latin American revolutionaries. We are grateful to you and your people for the example of unshakable fortitude, readiness to win, and staunch dignity in the face of U.S. imperialism, the most powerful enemy of all peoples, including the people of the United States.

The message concludes by saluting the Cuban people as "healthy, educated, revolutionary and internationalist." That is why Cuba remains the target of U.S. aggression and why we see pictures like the one in yesterday's *New York Times*, which shows well fed and well dressed Cuban children digging trenches in which the Cuban people hope they will survive the U.S. attack they fear is imminent.

The Economic Blockade and the U.S. Destabilization Program

Testimony of Terence Cannon

Fellow at the Center for Legal Education and Urban Policy at the City College of New York and author of Revolutionary Cuba *(1981).*

The United States has been waging an undeclared war against Cuba for a quarter of a century. This war basically has two fronts. The first is an economic blockade; the second is military intervention, direct and indirect.

The purpose of this war has always been the same: to bend, cripple and, if possible, destroy the Cuban Revolution. That policy has not changed since the war began twenty-five years ago. Cuba's aim has been economic and political independence. The consistent objective of the U.S. administration has been to restore U.S. economic and political dominance over Cuba, its economy and its people.

How did this begin? Listen to the words of the U.S. president, Dwight D. Eisenhower, who was in office when it all began.

> Within a matter of weeks after Castro entered Havana, we in the administration informally began to examine measures that might be effective in restraining Castro if he should develop into a menace. One suggestion was that we begin to build up an anti-Castro force within the island itself. Some thought we should quarantine the island, arguing that if the Cuban economy declined sharply, Cubans themselves would overthrow Castro.
>
> On March 17, 1960, I ordered the CIA to begin to organize the training of Cuban exiles, mainly in Guatemala.

Note several things about this statement: first, the utter willingness to use starvation and economic deprivation to bring the Cuban people to heel; second, the fear that this tiny island with its six million people would "develop into a menace" to the United States; and third, the willingness to organize inside Cuba to try to overthrow its government. The statement reveals the U.S. government's utter contempt for self-government, self-determination, and international peace.

Note also the date: March 17, 1960. At that point no U.S. properties had been nationalized; no Soviet oil was coming to Cuba; Cuba was not trading with socialist nations; Cuba had not established diplomatic relations with the Soviet Union; Cuba had not sent any troops to foreign countries and was not supporting revolutions in Latin America. Nevertheless, President Eisenhower ordered the CIA to begin overthrowing the Cuban government.

In fact, the campaign began even earlier. In June 1959 the first small planes started crossing the Florida Straits to bomb and strafe Cuban sugar mills and plantations.

In October 1959 the infamous Major Huber Matos, acting in league with the landowners of Camaguey Province, tried to turn a section of the rebel army against the revolution. (I must say that the recent emergence of Matos as a democratic prisoner of conscience can only be treated as some kind of right-wing joke.)

A few days later Havana was bombed and strafed. Eleven years later we came to know very well the copilot of the plane that attacked Havana. He was Frank Sturgis, later involved in the Watergate caper.

On March 4, 1960, a French ship was blown up in the Havana harbor, killing almost a hundred people. Two weeks later Eisenhower ordered the CIA to begin the overthrow of the Cuban government.

In the first few months of 1960 the United States began to withdraw exports, technology, spare parts, machinery, publications, information — everything they could to try to cripple the Cuban economy.

You have to understand the extraordinary level of dependence that had developed, based on hundreds of years of utter colonial status. The smallest spare part in Cuba at that time came from Miami. The Cubans didn't even have warehouses in Havana for most types of spare parts. Why should they? They could call up Miami, and what they needed would come over on the ferry a few hours later. Machinery and spare parts were all made in the United States.

At first the United States assumed that it would not take much effort to bring Cuba to heel. Fidel Castro, being just another *caudillo*, would realize the lack of wisdom in his revolution and come crawling back to the United States.

Instead, Cuba, in defense of its sovereignty, began to diversify its markets. In May 1960 Cuba signed its first trade agreement with the Soviet Union. Basically, the Soviet Union provided oil, and Cuba provided sugar in return. This was an unprecedented kind of trade agreement for Cuba. She no longer had to pay in dollars but could pay with sugar. It was a dream come true for Cuba. (Cuba, by the way, has not a drop of oil of its own. All the oil Cuba uses has to be imported from abroad.)

Cuba naturally asked the three companies that owned oil refineries in Cuba — which just happened to be Texaco, Standard Oil, and Shell — to refine the imported Soviet oil. The companies refused, so the Cuban government nationalized the refineries.

After the nationalization of the refineries in 1960, Eisenhower cut the U.S. sugar quota (a guarantee that the United States would buy a certain amount of sugar from Cuba each year) by 700,000 tons, thus eliminating in a single stroke 95 percent of the market for all the sugar Cuba had left to sell that year. To a small country like Cuba, dependent on a single crop like sugar, this was a devastating blow.

At that point Fidel told the crowd in Havana, "If they take away our quota pound by pound, we will take away their sugar mills one by one." In fact, he accelerated the nationalization program and took over all the sugar mills at once. In August 1960 the Cuban government nationalized all U.S. holdings in Cuba, amounting to about two billion dollars worth of major infrastructure.

On January 3, 1961, Eisenhower broke diplomatic relations with Cuba and ended all trade relations between the two countries. Three weeks later John F. Kennedy became president. Fidel Castro offered to negotiate, and we all know what happened next.

On April 17, 1961, an invading force of fifteen hundred – organized, supported, armed, transported, and treated like fools by the U.S. Central Intelligence Agency – attacked at the Bay of Pigs. Seventy-two hours later it was all over – the first and most humiliating defeat for imperialism in the Americas.

The subsequent attacks by the U.S. government were basically twofold. First, the United States sought to isolate Cuba diplomatically and expel her from the Organization of American States (OAS). That took a while, but this was eventually accomplished. Second, the United States established an embargo on all trade to and from Cuba; not only from the United States, which Eisenhower had already done, but from the rest of the "free world."

Fidel described the economic effects of the embargo in simple terms:

> We need steel, but we have no steel. We need tin, but we have no tin. We need ships, but we have neither the steel with which to build the ships, nor the technicians, engineers and specialists. We have no chemical products for food preservation. We have to import all this from one place or another. We need paint to paint the tin, and we have neither the paint nor the technique nor the machines with which to do it.

Almost 100 percent of the raw materials used in Cuba's factories came from the United States, and the equipment was adapted to operate with those raw materials. Overnight the United States prohibited the sale of those raw materials to Cuba.

Not only did the United States ban the export of raw materials and spare parts from the United States to Cuba, but it also prohibited other countries from selling anything to Cuba that contained anything made in the United States or anything on which a U.S. citizen held a patent. No contract was too small to escape examination by the U.S. Department of Commerce. Like private detectives, they went out all over the world, examining every line in every contract between Cuba and other countries, making sure that the contract covered nothing that was made in the United States or patented by a U.S. citizen.

For instance, Cuba had signed a contract with a British firm to build a much-needed fertilizer complex in Cuba. The United States prevented the company from using any U.S.-made or -patented parts in that fertilizer complex, even down to screws, nuts, and bolts. The British company had to search in dozens of countries to find equivalent parts on which patents were not held by U.S. citizens.

Needless to say, these measures did not succeed. Capitalists, being what they are, did not want to lose a lucrative market in Cuba. So European businessmen did not go along with the embargo. This was particularly true of the Scandinavian countries, which maintained and even increased their aid to Cuba after the embargo was imposed.

But the main thrust of Cuba's method of dealing with the embargo was to expand enormously their trade with the socialist countries. In 1959 these countries made up 2.2 percent of Cuba's foreign trade. This rose to 24 percent in 1960, 70 percent in 1961, and 80 percent in 1962.

How was the blockade overcome? Basically, it was overcome in three ways. The first two factors we have already discussed: Many capitalist countries refused to join in the embargo, and Cuba's trade was reoriented toward the socialist camp. The third important factor was the daily individual heroism of the Cuban people. I remember I once had a chauffeur who had the hood of his car open and was tinkering with the engine. It was a 1959 Cadillac, but it had a Czechoslovakian starter motor and a Bulgarian battery. He had reamed out the cylinders so he could fit in pistons from Rumania. The car was like a miniature United Nations.

That was how the Cubans kept their cars and their other machines going for twenty years, using whatever they could get. The same thing happened in the factories. The workers had to fabricate spare parts and learn almost everything from scratch.

Today we can say that the blockade is no longer a major threat to Cuba's economic existence. However, it has slowed Cuba's rate of growth and hampered Cuba's ability to provide a higher standard of living and more consumer goods for her people. The Cuban people continue to live in economic conditions below those that would exist if there were no blockade.

The second front in the U.S. war against Cuba is military intervention. The U.S.-sponsored campaign of sabotage, armed attacks, terrorism, destabilization, murders, bombings, torture, and assassinations is truly unprecedented, and most of the campaign has been conducted under strict U.S. government control.

In 1960 and 1961 there were thirty-four armed interventions involving thirteen ships. From 1962 to 1965 a major war raged in the Escambray Mountains, with counterrevolutionary bands organized, trained, supplied, and paid for by the CIA. More Cubans died fighting the counterrevolutionaries in Escambray that died as combatants in the revolutionary war.

From 1960 to 1965 the CIA was involved in at least eight attempts to kill Castro. Fidel submitted a list of twenty-four plots to the Church Subcommittee of the Senate, but the committee was able to confirm only eight. Most of these plots involved Mafiosi, who had helped run Cuba, especially the tourist trade, until the triumph of the Revolution and who therefore knew their way around.

The plots involved long-range rifles, poison pills, poison cigars, poison ballpoint pens, powders containing deadly bacteria, LSD, chemicals to make Fidel's beard fall out, and booby-trapped sea shells designed to be placed where Castro went diving. Some of this may just seem ludicrous at this point, but you can imagine how the United States would have reacted if some foreign country tried to kill our president even once, let alone if it conducted such a concerted effort.

The recent trial of the Omega 7 leader shows that the assassinations, shootings, and bombings all are still going on.

The terror machine created by the United States has resulted in countless murders of civilians in Cuba and in the United States. It is connected with the murder in Washington, D.C., of Orlando Letelier, the former ambassador from Chile; the murder in New York City of a Cuban diplomat; and the murders of Cuban-Americans who favor dialogue with the Cuban government. The United States continues to foster terrorist groups among exiles from Cuba.

In order to show the continuity of U.S. policy over time, let me quote the U.S. Secretary of State:

> The Communists' favorite slogan is: "Yankee, go home!" Why any American would wish to further that central Communist objective is beyond my comprehension.
>
> In October we embargoed exports to Nicaragua, excepting foodstuffs and medicine. These actions were taken for very good reasons. There will be no retreat from our policy toward the Sandinista regime in Nicaragua because we regard this regime as temporary. We expect the Nicaragua people to regain their freedom and rejoin the inter-American system.
>
> The free nations who sell to Nicaragua goods and equipment important to the Nicaragua economy are interfering with the efforts of the free nations of this hemisphere to curb this danger.

This is precisely the policy enunciated last week by [George] Shultz and the U.S. government. However, these words were not spoken by Mr. Shultz. I changed all the names in order to make a point. They were spoken by Dean Rusk in 1964, and he was talking about Cuba.

U.S.-Imposed Limitations on the Right to Travel and on Information

Testimony of Harold Mayerson

Attorney with the law firm of Mayerson, Zorn and Smith and currently representing Marazul Tours, which is being investigated by the U.S. Justice Department because it organizes tours to Cuba.

My task is to cover the modern period of Cuban-American relations: that is, the period since 1977, roughly speaking.

Terry Cannon just said that the United States has been waging an undeclared war against the people of Cuba. I would say that the United States has been waging two Cuba-related wars for the last twenty-five years, and the second war is against the U.S. people. I think the events of the last seven years, and of the last several months in particular, demonstrate that without question. I say that because in the last seven years the U.S. government has taken actions that directly infringe on the rights of all U.S. citizens. They have done this in a number of ways.

Relations between the United States and Cuba are governed in large part by the Cuban Foreign Assets Control Regulations, which were promulgated pursuant to the Trading with the Enemy Act. We say that the modern period in Cuban–U.S. relations started in 1977 because that spring the Carter administration made two substantial changes in those regulations.

First, the new regulations permitted "persons subject to U.S. jurisdiction" (the precise phrase is important legally) to travel to Cuba and spend money there for food and lodging and other travel expenses. Secondly, they also permitted U.S. travel agencies to make travel arrangements for people going to Cuba.

Many people viewed these changes as a liberalization, an expansion of our right to travel and our right to learn about the world through personal experience, an enhancement of the free flow of information about the world. While the new regulations did in fact have this effect to a certain degree, I doubt that this was the Carter administration's main motivation. Rather, the change was the administration's response to the strong lobbying campaigns being conducted at the time by U.S. corporate interests and U.S. allies on the one hand, and by Cuban-Americans on the other.

Under the pre-1977 regulations foreign subsidiaries of U.S. multinational corporations were not free to trade with Cuba. These subsidiaries wanted to do business with Cuba, and they therefore lobbied to have the regulations changed. So did their parent companies, and so did the foreign countries (such U.S. allies as Canada and Argentina) where the subsidiaries were based.

Another source of lobbying on this issue was the legitimate and pent-up demand by Cuban-Americans who wanted to return to Cuba to visit their relatives and had been unable to do so legally for almost two decades. If you look at who has traveled to Cuba from the United States since 1977, probably 95 percent have been Cuban-Americans going there to visit their families.

But whatever the motivations of the Carter administration, the changes in the regulations led to a five-year period during which travel to Cuba was more open than at any other time since the Revolution came to power.

The next significant event in this story occurred in the spring of 1980, when a group of Cubans sought asylum in the Peruvian embassy in Havana. The U.S. presidential election campaign was in progress, and Carter was competing with Reagan for the votes of conservatives, including conservative Cubans in Florida. As a result, Carter told Castro, "We will take all the people who want to leave." The Castro government responded, "If you want them, you can have them." Many of the would-be exiles took advantage of this offer and came to the United States in the operation that came to be known as the Mariel boatlift.

As a consequence of Mariel, the U.S. Department of the Treasury, which enforces the foreign-assets control regulations, began to investigate the travel agencies that arrange travel to Cuba. The investigation, which began under the Carter administration, continued under the Reagan administration and did not result in an indictment until the spring of 1982. My sense of what was happening during much of that time was that the Reagan administration was trying to decide what it was going to do about Cuba.

In the meantime the Reagan administration did take one action related to Cuba, an action that probably seemed minor from their point of view but had a significant impact on the U.S. left. In the spring of 1981 the Reagan administration stopped the delivery of printed material originating in Cuba.

There was a lawsuit to protest that action, supported by the Center for Constitutional Rights, the American Civil Liberties Union, and the Emergency Civil Liberties Committee. The lawsuit was successful. But a lot of energy was expended by many political people and lawyers just to win back rights that never should have been taken away in the first place.

This action by the Reagan administration was a clear instance of the war being waged against the U.S. people. The financial impact of the decision on Cuba was so slight that it's not worth discussing. The only point of the action was to prevent us from receiving information from Cuba.

In the spring of 1982 the Reagan administration took a major step toward suppressing or chilling the comparatively free travel to Cuba that had been going on since the 1977 liberalization. There was only one U.S. company that operated charter flights to Cuba, a Florida company called American Airway Charters, and the government decided to put it out of business.

They designated the company a foreign national; that is, they said it was really a Cuban company and not a U.S. company and was therefore not permitted to do business in the United States. They also froze and took over the company's assets, and they indicted virtually everybody involved in the company for violating the foreign-assets control regulations.

I want to tell you about one of those cases in some detail, so you get a flavor of what the government is up to here. My law firm is representing Fred Fuentes, a Cuban-American who is the president of American Airway Charters. He was convicted of violating the Trading with the Enemy Act in what amounted to a kangaroo court in Miami. Specifically, his alleged violations consisted of delivering the following items to Cuba: some ham and cheese sandwiches, some whiskey, four Pepsi machines, a small airplane part, and some quarters to be used at the airport to make change.

He was sentenced to spend one year in the penitentiary. We appealed his conviction to the Eleventh Circuit, but it was affirmed. We filed a petition for rehearing and are now waiting for the court's response. If these appeals are unsuccessful, Fred Fuentes will have to serve his time, and I believe he will be a true political prisoner.

My law firm was also asked to represent the charter company itself, and we agreed to do so. The next thing I knew a government agent called me and told me we couldn't represent the charter company because we needed a special license to represent a designated foreign national. We already knew that there was a special regulation about representing designated foreign nationals: That regulation said that a lawyer representing a designated foreign national had to get government permission to get paid. Now it turned out that the Reagan administration had adopted a new regulation that required government permission not only to get paid, but even to undertake the representation.

We felt this new regulation was an unprecedented restriction on people's freedom to pick their own lawyer, and we challenged the regulation in court. We lost in the district court, and that case is now pending before the D.C. Circuit; they've been sitting on it for four months. If this case is not reversed, it will serve as the first partial precedent for the proposition that the government has the right to decide who your lawyer is going to be.

[Editor's note: Fred Fuentes lost his appeal before the Eleventh Circuit, and the U.S. Supreme Court has declined to hear his case. However, on the issue of licensing lawyers, Mr. Mayerson won a reversal by the D.C. Circuit.]

To return to our main theme, the Reagan administration this past July rewrote the regulations governing travel to Cuba and made them much more restrictive. Basically, the government said that the only categories of people who can go to Cuba and spend money there are people with relatives in Cuba and certain types of intellectuals, such as journalists or researchers who are going to Cuba as part of their work.

Again, we brought a lawsuit to challenge these regulations, arguing that Congress had not given the President the unilateral right to prevent people from traveling to Cuba. That case, known as *Reagan v. Wald*, 104 S.Ct. 3026 (1984), went all the way to the U.S. Supreme Court, which decided against us this past June. It was a five-to-four decision, and many commentators have criticized the decision as quite muddled in its thinking and as having been dictated by the political desire to uphold the imperial presidency—that is, the right of the President to make decisions that go against the law.

We believe that the financial impact of these new regulations on Cuba are slight and that the Reagan administration's real purpose in making these changes was to restrict the right of U.S. citizens to travel to Cuba and learn about conditions there on their own.

Under the regulations, if you are a lawyer who wants to study Cuba's legal system, or an academic who wants to study the Cuban health system, or a professional journalist who wants to cover some news item down there, you can go. But God forbid if you are a trade unionist who wants to see how the Federation of Cuban Workers functions. That is not allowed. And God forbid if you are a black person who wants to learn about how Cuba has dealt with racism. Unless you are a professional, that is not allowed. God forbid if you are a Christian who is interested in the church in Cuba and in liberation theology. Unless you are a professional, you can't go. God forbid if you like Cuban music. Unless you are a professional critic or musicologist, you can't go. God forbid if you want to relax on the beach and sunbathe— and Cuba has a lot of sun and many beautiful beaches. Again, you can't go.

To give a complete picture of U.S.-Cuban relations, we would have to discuss at least two other matters: First, in the spring of 1983 the Reagan administration designated Prensa Latina (a Canadian company reporting news in the United States) a Cuban national and kicked it out of the country—this at a time when the administration was complaining about the allegedly anti-free-press policies of UNESCO [United Nations Educational, Scientific, and Cultural Organization] and many Third World countries. Second, the Reagan administration has fairly consistently denied visas to Cubans who have been invited to the United States to speak here, which once again shows the administration's intention to cut off our access to information about Cuba.

Several months ago the U.S. government once again made a major move. They served a series of subpoenas on a New York travel agency, Marazul Tours, ordering Marazul to produce all its books, records, and accounts relating to travel to Cuba. It was not by chance that they picked on Marazul. Of the three companies that send planes to Cuba, Marazul is the smallest and sends the fewest passengers to Cuba. But they send the largest number of passengers in the intellectual categories, such as academics and journalists. The government was asking not only for the names of people who went to Cuba; they were even asking for the names of people who had just been sent a brochure. They wanted to be able to send those people a letter telling them they shouldn't go to Cuba.

The response of the press was astounding, even the generally conservative press. When even the *Washington Post* says that we are returning to a period of McCarthyism, you know that something is seriously wrong.

I think that what we have to deal with here is more than just a narrow legal issue for lawyers to work on. It's a political challenge for all of us to work on: namely, how do we counteract the two wars that are going on, the war against Cuba, and the war being waged against the U.S. people and the U.S. Constitution?

Conclusions of Law

The actions of the Reagan administration with respect to Cuba violate the following provisions of law:

1. Its obligation under the Charter of the Organization of American States (article 19) and under customary international law, as evidenced by General Assembly Resolutions 2131 (1965) (Declaration on the Inadmissibility of Intervention in the Domestic Affairs of States), 2625 (1970) (Declaration on Principles of International Law Concerning Friendly Relations and Cooperation Among States), and 3281 (1974) (Charter of the Economic Rights and Duties of States), to refrain from using "coercive measures of an economic or political character in order to force the sovereign will of another state and obtain from it advantages of any kind."

2. Its obligation under the General Agreement on Tariffs and Trade (GATT) to refrain from manipulating export and import controls in a retaliatory fashion.

3. Its obligation under customary international law to refrain from drastic economic reprisals such as blockades unless (a) negotiations first prove fruitless, and (b) the reprisal is proportionate to the harm suffered by the party imposing the blockade.

Conclusion

The Reagan administration's foreign policy in Central America and the Caribbean threatens our constitutional form of government and has created a serious threat to international peace and security. The appropriate response to this threat is the imposition of enforcement measures by the United Nations Security Council under articles 41 and 42 of the United Nations Charter.

In the event that the Reagan administration exercises its veto power against the adoption of such measures by the Security Council, the matter should be turned over to the United Nations General Assembly for action in accordance with the procedures set forth in the United for Peace Resolution of 1950. In this manner the serious violations of international law being committed by the United States could be effectively opposed by all members of the world community in a manner consistent with the requirements of international law.

Appendixes

Appendix A:
Statement of Purpose

Whereas sufficient preliminary evidence exists to indicate that the U.S. government has conducted its foreign policy in Central America and the Caribbean in violation of international and domestic law, and accepted customs, in that:

- it is steadily escalating an overt and covert war against the people of Nicaragua:
- it continues to support the governments of Guatemala, Honduras, El Salvador which have been responsible for systematic human rights abuses:
- it invaded and continues to occupy the island of Grenada:
- it ignores the opinion of the American people and refuses to submit its actions to the jurisdiction of the World Court:

Whereas these and other acts threaten to become a regional war that endangers all peoples of the world:

Whereas domestic U.S. courts have failed to examine the legality of U.S. military actions in Central America and the Caribbean:

Whereas the established media of this country have declined to present a full and fair picture of the situation in the region:

Be it resolved that we, the citizens of the United States, are therefore prepared to accept the responsibility of conducting War Crimes Tribunals which shall:

- examine the legality of the U.S. government's activities throughout Central America and the Caribbean, as well as its refusal to submit its actions to the judgment of the International Court of Justice, the United Nations or any other appropriate international or domestic body:
- present a forum where U.S. citizens and victims of U.S. military and covert actions in Central America and the Caribbean can document the human suffering caused by these activities:
- hear relevant evidence of alleged violations of U.S. and international law, and accepted customs and to bring this evidence before a wide spectrum of the public:
- awaken the public conscience of the people of the United States in order to insure that the U.S. government adheres to the fundamental principles of international law and morality.

Appendix B:
War Crimes Tribunal
Indictment

THE PEOPLE OF THE
UNITED STATES OF
AMERICA,

       Plaintiffs,

  — against —

RONALD WILSON REAGAN,
President of the
United States of America;
WILLIAM CASEY, Director of
the Central Intelligence Agency;
GEORGE P. SHULTZ, Secretary
of State;
CASPAR WEINBERGER,
Secretary of Defense;
and Unnamed Executive Officials
of the
Administration of President
Reagan,

       Defendants.

COUNT ONE: PLANNING AND WAGING AGGRESSIVE WAR IN CENTRAL AMERICA AND THE CARIBBEAN

The people of the United States charge:

1. From on or about January 20, 1981, continuing to the present time, in the United States of America and in the countries of Central America, the Caribbean and elsewhere, Ronald Wilson Reagan, William Casey, George P. Shultz, Caspar Weinberger, the defendants, and other unnamed officials of

the Reagan administration ("co-conspirators"), unlawfully conspired to commit Crimes Against Peace and Crimes Against the Rules of War in violation of the Charter of the International Military Tribunal Act at Nuremberg, the United Nations Charter, the Charter of the Organization of American States, various treaties and the domestic laws of the United States including the Constitution thereof, the Neutrality Act (18 USC §960), and laws prohibiting aid to countries involved in gross violations of internationally recognized human rights.

OBJECT AND MEANS OF THE CONSPIRACY

2. The object of the conspiracy planned and carried out by the defendants and their co-conspirators is the overthrow of the government of Nicaragua, the violent suppression of peoples' struggles for self-determination in El Salvador and Guatemala, the overthrow of the government of Grenada and the occupation of that country, the military control of Honduras and continued U.S. domination and control of the countries of Central America and the Caribbean. Among the means by which defendants and their co-conspirators carry out their conspiracy are the preparation, releasing, launching, and waging of wars of aggression, the aiding and abetting of such wars of aggression, the spreading of terror among the civilian population, economic sabotage and economic and political measures meant to coerce the sovereign rights of the countries of the Caribbean and Central America.

OVERT ACTS

3. In furtherance of said conspiracy to effect its objects, the following overt acts among others were committed in the United States and in the countries of Central America, the Caribbean and elsewhere:

NICARAGUA

a. The defendants are recruiting, paying, equipping, supplying, training, and directing a paramilitary mercenary force of more than 10,000 men against the peoples and government of Nicaragua. This force is ravaging the civilian population, attempting to destroy Nicaragua's economy and overthrow its government;

b. These paramilitary forces funded, trained, and directed by the defendants have engaged in numerous acts of torture, rape, kidnapping and summary executions against the people of Nicaragua; this has resulted in the deaths of more than 1400 Nicaraguans, military personnel and civilians, serious injury to more than 1700 others and $200,000,000 in direct damage to property. Many of these attacks are aimed at indigenous peoples, health care workers, schoolteachers and priests. Health clinics, schools, and daycare centers in border areas are targeted and destroyed;

c. The activities of the defendants are part of a continuing and organized use of force that since its inception in 1981 has steadily expanded. In March, 1984, 6,000 U.S.-backed mercenaries initiated the largest assault to date on Nicaraguan territory. Heavy fighting is continuing and casualties are high;

d. Defendants have mined the Nicaraguan ports of Corinto, Sandino and El Bluff, causing extensive damage to the life and economy of Nicaragua and infringing on the freedom of the high seas and maritime commerce. Taken together with the previous bombings of Managua's international airport, these actions not only attempt to cut off Nicaragua's vital trade and communications with the world, but constitute a mortal hazard to third parties engaged in peaceful international commerce and travel;

e. The defendants have directed the bombing of the oil storage facilities of Puerto Corinto and other facilities, causing grave risk to and disruption of human life and damaging the economy of Nicaragua;

f. The above-described war is and was engaged in without the constitutionally-required assent of the Congress of the United States, in violation of the United States Constitution, Article I, Section 8, clause 11, and the Neutrality Act, 18 U.S.C. §960, which prohibits the launching of armed expeditions or wars against countries with which the United States is at peace. Violations of the Neutrality Act are punishable by three years of imprisonment. The United Nations Charter, Article (2)(4) prohibits the "threat or use of force against the territorial integrity or political independence of any state. . . ." Numerous other international instruments establish the prohibition on arming of groups or irregular forces to carry out acts of aggression against another state. At Nuremberg, the United States and other powers recognized that aggression is a crime for which the individuals responsible should be prosecuted. These acts also violate fundamental human rights provisions which must be enforced in all circumstances, e.g., Declaration on Protection of All Persons From Being Subjected to Torture and Other Cruel, Inhuman or Degrading Treatment or Punishment.

EL SALVADOR

g. The defendants are providing funding, weapons, training and direction to the military forces of the government of El Salvador, a government involved in a consistent pattern of gross violations of internationally recognized human rights. That government has been responsible for the deaths of over 40,000 innocent civilians. Many of these deaths have been caused by death squads operated by the government of El Salvador with the connivance of the defendants. Those not killed instantly have been subjected to torture or cruel and degrading treatment, prolonged detention without charges, disappearances, and other flagrant denial of the right to life and family. Nations are prohibited by both international law and U.S. law from directly or indirectly engaging in any actions that cause the deprivation of human rights. The United Nations Charter, the Universal Declaration of Human Rights, and the American Convention on Human Rights require that all members promote a universal respect for human rights. The Foreign Assistance Act of 1961, as amended, specifically prohibits U.S. military or economic aid to any country which engages in a consistent pattern of gross violations of internationally recognized human rights. 21 U.S.C. §2151; 22 U.S.C. §2304;

h. Defendants are providing aerial reconnaissance for the Salvadoran air force which results in the indiscriminate bombing and killing of civilian populations in El Salvador;

i. Defendants are supplying napalm and phosphorus weapons to the government of El Salvador for use in bombing populated areas, causing non-combatant injuries and aggravated suffering;

j. Defendants have sent at least fifty members of the armed forces to El Salvador who are fighting side by side with government forces, contrary to the requirements of the War Powers Resolution, which mandate Congressional approval of the use of such armed forces;

k. Defendants have staged and manipulated an election in El Salvador, which does not express the will of the people. The FDR/FMLN could not participate in the election; the population was coerced into participation, and state-sponsored terrorism prevented organizing and campaigning for opponents of the government. The U.S. supported with direct financial aid the candidacy of José Napoleón Duarte;

l. Thousands of refugees have fled El Salvador for fear of being prosecuted or killed by the government. Defendants, contrary to international and domestic law, have denied these refugees their right to apply for and obtain political asylum. Many refugees have been coerced by defendants to return to El Salvador where they face death or imprisonment. The 1951 Convention relating to the status of refugees and the 1967 Protocol thereto, among others, prohibit states from returning refugees to a place of persecution and requires the granting of at least temporary asylum.

GRENADA

m. On October 25, 1981, the defendants prepared, launched, and waged aggressive war against the people and government of Grenada. Over 5,000 U.S. armed forces were in the invasion force, which resulted in the deaths of 161 Grenadians and wounding of 100, the deaths of 71 Cubans and the wounding of 57. The defendants continue to maintain an occupation force of 300, and 100 "trainers". Prior to the invasion, the defendants made repeated efforts to destabilize the government of Grenada, strangle the country economically, and at least three years earlier prepared a plan for conquest.

HONDURAS

n. The defendants have constructed airfields, ammunition dumps, radar facilities, conducted training exercises, and permanently stationed at least 700 U.S. armed forces in Honduras in preparation for a war of aggression against the people of Central America and particularly Nicaragua and El Salvador. These preparations have been made contrary to both domestic and international law. The War Powers Resolution prohibits increasing U.S. armed forces in a country without compliance with its provisions requiring a report to Congress. It further requires Congressional approval if U.S. forces are involved in hostilities or face imminent hostilities. The building of permanent facilities in Honduras was done fraudulently with monies not appropriated for that purpose.

o. On or about March, 1984, defendants directed U.S. armed forces to operate surveillance flights from Honduras against the people of El Salvador. Said flights targeted civilian areas and directed two El Salvadoran planes on bombing raids, causing the deaths of scores if not hundreds of innocent Salvadoran citizens.

CUBA

p. Defendants, contrary to international law, continue to maintain an economic blockade of Cuba, assert ownership over part of the sovereign territory of Cuba (Guantanamo), fly espionage flights over Cuba, and commit acts of sabotage on the island. Soon defendants will begin broadcasting propaganda into Cuban territory. Defendants have unconstitutionally limited the rights of U.S. citizens to travel freely to Cuba.

THE PEOPLE OF THE UNITED STATES CHARGE: Crimes Against Peace and Crimes Against the Rules of War are charges of the utmost gravity. Such wars of aggression and war crimes are the supreme international crimes.

prepared by: Michael Ratner
Anne Simon
Center for Constitutional
Rights
853 Broadway
New York, New York 10003

Appendix C:
Judges of the Tribunal

REVEREND BEN CHAVIS is an ordained minister of the United Church of Christ and deputy director of its Commission for Racial Justice. He is a twenty-one-year veteran of the civil-rights movement, and has worked with Dr. Martin Luther King, Jr., the Southern Christian Leadership Conference, and the NAACP. The recipient of numerous human rights awards, he spent four and a half years in prison as one of the Wilmington Ten, whose unjust convictions were overturned in December 1980 by the United States Court of Appeals for the Fourth Circuit.

STANLEY FAULKNER is an international lawyer practicing in New York City. He was a member of the Law Commission of the Bertrand Russell International War Crimes Tribunal on Vietnam and adviser to the presiding judge of that tribunal. He was also a member of the International Jurists Commission on Apartheid and was awarded the Peace Medal of the German Democratic Republic in 1976. Mr. Faulkner was also associate defense counsel for David Siqueiros, the Mexican artist, in 1962 and associate defense counsel for Chilean political prisoners in 1974. Mr. Faulkner is presiding judge of the tribunal.

PAUL O'DWYER was president of the New York City Council from 1974 to 1978 and was active in New York City politics for many years. He was president of the New York City chapter of the National Lawyers Guild in 1948 and has defended many political prisoners, including—during the Franco era—the Carabanchel Ten, a group of labor leaders convicted for joining an independent trade union. In recent years Mr. O'Dwyer has been active in the cause for the independence of Northern Ireland.

ROSA PARKS started the famous bus boycott in Montgomery, Alabama, on December 1, 1955, which lasted for 365 days. Ms. Parks would like it to be known that her refusal to move to the back of the bus was not a spontaneous decision, but one made after a lifetime, since the age of four, of awareness of the horrors of Jim Crow and its humiliating effects on black people. Ms. Parks is a national hero to several generations of people whom she inspired to work in the civil-rights movement, and she continues today to inspire all people who work for social justice. She is the recipient of many humanitarian awards and currently serves as adviser to the Congressional Black Caucus.

WILMA REVERON-TÍO is an attorney who was active in the student movement at the University of Puerto Rico from 1970 to 1974. In 1979 she became involved in the struggle against the U.S. Navy's use of the island of Vieques for maneuvers and target practice; she was arrested for and ultimately acquitted of trespassing on a military installation. She is now executive director of the Office of International Information for the Independence of Puerto Rico, a United Nations lobbying organization. She is also assistant professor of Puerto Rican studies at the City University of New York and coordinator of the Comité Lares of the United Nations, a broad coalition of supporters of Puerto Rican independence in the United States.

DORIS TURNER is president of Local 1199 of the National Union of Hospital and Health Care Employees Union, RWDSU, AFL-CIO. Active in the civil-rights and other social-justice movements for many years, she is presently serving on two New York State councils — the Hospital Review and Planning Council and the AIDS Council. She is also chairperson and fundraiser for the Harlem YM/YWCA and has been for many years a director of the Martin Luther King, Jr., Center for Nonviolent Social Change in Atlanta.

HONORABLE BRUCE McM. WRIGHT, a justice of the New York State Supreme Court, began his judicial career when he was appointed to the Criminal Court by Mayor John Lindsay. In 1979 he was elected to the Civil Court, where he served until his election to the Supreme Court in 1982. A published poet, Judge Wright also serves on the boards of the Fortune Society, the NAACP, the Asian-American Legal Defense Fund, and other organizations. He is the recipient of numerous humanitarian awards, including Judge of the Year from the National Bar Association.

Appendix D: Legal Secretariat

MARTIN POPPER, Chairperson, is an attorney with, and senior partner of, Wolf, Popper, Ross, Wolf & Jones; the vice-president of the Consular Law Society; and a member of the New York Bar. He was a consultant to the U.S. delegation to the founding conference of the United Nations; an official observer to the International War Crimes Tribunal at Nuremberg; and executive secretary of the National Lawyers Guild.

RAFAEL ANGLADA-LÓPEZ is a recent law graduate and staff member at the Center for Constitutional Rights and a former journalist in Puerto Rico. He recently attended the International Progress Organization Tribunal on the Foreign Policy of the Reagan Administration in Brussels, Belgium.

JUAN CARTAGENA is a staff attorney with the Puerto Rican Legal Defense and Education Fund and a member of the New York Bar and the New Jersey Bar.

RICHARD HARVEY is an attorney practicing with the Harlem-based law firm of Stevens, Hinds & White; a delegate of the International Association of Democratic Lawyers to the United Nations; a barrister-at-law in England and Wales; and a member of the New York Bar.

JULES LOBEL is a professor of international law at the University of Pittsburgh Law School; a cooperating attorney with the Center for Constitutional Rights; a member of the National Lawyers Guild; and a member of the New York Bar. He is a counsel in *Dellums v. Smith*.

CATHY POTLER is an attorney with the Correctional Association, defending prisoners' rights; a member of the Executive Committee of the National Lawyers Guild, New York City Chapter; and a member of the New York Bar. She has visited Central America recently.

PAUL RAMSHAW is a volunteer attorney at the Center for Constitutional Rights; a member of the National Lawyers Guild; and a member of the California Bar.

JUDY RABINOVITZ is a third-year law student at New York University Law School; an intern at the Center for Constitutional Rights; and a member of the National Lawyers Guild. She spent this past summer in Nicaragua documenting human-rights abuses by the contras.

MICHAEL SCHNEIDER is an attorney with the Legal Aid Society of Nassau County; a member of the Central America Task Force of the National Lawyers Guild; a member of the New York Bar; and a member of the Massachusetts Bar.

ADRIEN WING is an attorney specializing in international law at Curtis, Mallet-Prevost, Colt and Mosley; is a National Conference of Black Lawyers delegate to the United Nations. She traveled in Nicaragua, Cuba, and Grenada in July 1983 with a congressional delegation.

SARAH WUNSCH is an attorney with the Center for Constitutional Rights and a member of the New York Bar. She is a counsel in *Sánchez-Espinoza v. Reagan* and has traveled in Nicaragua in connection with her representation of Nicaraguan clients.

ELLEN YAROSHEFSKY is an attorney with the Center for Constitutional Rights; a chairperson of the Central America Task Force of the National Lawyers Guild; a member of the New York Bar; and a member of the State of Washington Bar. She is a counsel in *Sánchez-Espinoza v. Reagan* and in *Dellums v. Smith*.

Appendix E:
Program of the War Crimes Tribunal on Central America and the Caribbean, New York City

MONDAY, OCTOBER 8TH
COLUMBIA UNIVERSITY, SCHOOL OF INTERNATIONAL AFFAIRS,
KELLOGG CENTER, 420 W. 118TH ST., 15TH FLOOR.

Welcome.

Opening Statement by presiding judge.

Taking of the Evidence.
I. THE CONSPIRACY TO DENY THE PEOPLES OF THE REGION THEIR RIGHT TO SELF-DETERMINATION.
    A. Historical Overview
    B. Economic Dependency and Self-Determination
    C. Militarization of the Region
    Witnesses:
    Prof. Julio Quam, Executive Director of the Latin American Center of Friends World College, San Jose, Costa Rica.
    Prof. Saskia Sassen-Koob, Professor of Sociology, Queens College, the Graduate School, CUNY, and author of the forthcoming book, *The Foreign Investment Connection: Rethinking Immigration.*
    Robert Ostertag, editor of *The Alert!: Focus on Central America*, Committee in Solidarity with the People of El Salvador.
    Estela Vazquez, Dominican-born social worker; antiintervention activist.

II. U.S. SUPPORT OF GOVERNMENTS ENGAGED IN CONSIS-TENT PATTERNS OF GROSS VIOLATIONS OF INTERNATION-ALLY RECOGNIZED HUMAN RIGHTS.
    A. GUATEMALA
    1. Oral history by a victim of government atrocities.
    2. Overview of human rights violations by government forces.

3. Forms of U.S. intervention: 1954 to the present.
4. Displacement and the refugee crisis.

Witnesses:

Rigoberta Menchú, Indian leader from El Quiché Province, member of the Peasant Unity Committee, and a victim of government atrocities.

Raúl Molina, former Professor and Dean at the School of Engineering of the University of San Carlos, Guatemala, Rector of the University.

Frank LaRue, exiled Guatemalan labor lawyer with the National Confederation of Workers and with the National Committee of Trade Union Unity.

Eddie Fischer, Executive Director of Peace for Guatemala who has lived and worked in Central America from 1976–81.

B. HONDURAS
1. The military build-up and domestic repression.

Witnesses:

Leyda Barbieri, associate at Washington Office on Latin America, author of numerous articles on Honduras, has testified before Congressional hearings on the military build-up in Honduras.

C. EL SALVADOR
1. Background to the crisis: from the Matanza of '32 to the October '79 coup.
2. Profile of José Napoleón Duarte.
3. Demonstration elections as counterinsurgency.
4. Military attacks and death squad operations against the civilian population.
5. Torture, summary execution and government prisons.
6. Health effects of the war on women and children.
7. The airwar and the use of napalm, white phosphorus and other anti-personnel weapons.
8. The policy of displacement and the flight of refugees.
9. Other first-hand accounts.

Witnesses:

Robert Armstrong, Staff member of the North American Congress on Latin America and co-author of *El Salvador: The Face of Revolution*.

Dr. Tommie Sue Montgomery, Professor of Political Science at Dickinson College and author of *Revolution in El Salvador: Origin and Evolution* and numerous articles on the church in Central America.

Frank Brodhead, activist and co-author of *Demonstration Elections: U.S. Staged Elections in the Dominican Republic, Viet Nam and El Salvador.*

Secundino Ramírez, Representative of the El Salvador Human Rights Commission.

Ramón Flores, Salvadoran victim of death squad torture, in church sanctuary in New Jersey.

Joanne Palmisano, M.D., Professor in Department of Internal Medicine, State University of New York, Downstate Medical Center, and member of the Second Public Health Commission delegation to El Salvador in January, 1983.

Charles Clements, M.D. (video), Vietnam Veteran, Faculty member at Albert Einstein College of Medicine and at the Department of Social Medicine at Montefiore Medical Center, practiced medicine in FMLN-controlled territory in El Salvador in 1982–83.

Richard Alan White, member of the September, 1984 Medical Aid to El Salvador delegation and author of *The Morass: U.S. Intervention in Central America*, Senior Fellow at the Council on Hemispheric Affairs.

Fr. Henry Atkins, Jr., a founder of Witness for Peace, former missionary in Central America, including La Virtud refugee camp, Episcopalian Chaplain at Rutgers University, and active in the sanctuary movement.

Héctor Recinos, Jr., Salvadoran refugee, son of one of the "STECEL 10," imprisoned Salvadoran labor leaders.

SUMMATION

Including: U.S. Constitution; art. I, §8, cl. 11; War Powers Resolution, art. 4(a); Foreign Assistance Act, S502B(a)(2); International Security Development Act, of 1981, S728(b) and (d); U.N. Charter, arts. 1, 2(3), 33(1), 55, 56; O.A.S. Charter, arts. 3(g) 23; Charter of the International Military Tribunal at Nuremberg, art. 6(c); Geneva Convention (IV) Relative to the Protection of Civilians; U.N. Declaration on Human Rights; American Convention on Human Rights; U.N. Convention Relating to the Status of Refugees.

TUESDAY, OCTOBER 9th
RIVERSIDE CHURCH, ASSEMBLY HALL, 120th AT CLAREMONT AVE.

Welcome.
Opening Statement by presiding judge.

III. PLANNING AND WAGING AGGRESSIVE WARS, OVERT AND COVERT.

A. CUBA

1. Overview: from the Bay of Pigs to pending threats of invasion.
2. The economic blockade and the U.S. destabilization program.
3. U.S. imposed limitations on the right to travel and information.

Witnesses:

Jane Franklin, political researcher, co-editor of *Cuba Update*, author of *Cuban Foreign Relations, A Chronology: 1959–1982*.

Prof. Terence Cannon, Revson Fellow at the Center for Legal Education and Urban Policy at City College of New York and author of *Revolutionary Cuba* (1981).

Harold Mayerson, attorney with Mayerson, Zorn, and Smith, representing Marazul Tours, currently under investigation by the Justice Department regarding travel to Cuba.

B. GRENADA

1. Overview: prelude to the invasion.
2. U.S. policy and the invasion of October 25, 1983.
3. The political and the social effects of the ongoing U.S. occupation.

Witnesses:

Joachim Mark, Grenadian historian and author of numerous articles on the Caribbean and Latin America.

Hazel Ross, Legislative Liaison for Economic Affairs at TransAfrica, the Black American Foreign Lobby on Africa and the Caribbean.

Prof. Margarita Samad-Matías, Director of the Latin America and Caribbean Studies Program at City College of New York and member of the first fact-finding delegation after the invasion in November, 1983.

C. NICARAGUA

1. History of U.S. intervention from the rise of Somoza I to the fall of Somoza III.
2. Disregarding the will of Congress.
3. The CIA's fabrication of intelligence data.
4. Techniques of destabilization.
5. The effects of the war: economic destruction and human suffering, an overview.
6. First-hand accounts of contra attacks and destruction.
7. Health effects of the war; medical personnel and facilities as targets of contra attacks.

8. CIA manipulation of the Atlantic Coast populations.
Witnesses:
Salvador Orochena, Nicaraguan student leader, arrested and exiled by Somoza in 1971 and graduate of Antioch Law School.
David MacMichael, former CIA analyst on Central America, 1981–83.
William Schaap, Co-editor of *Covert Action* and cooperating attorney with the Center for Constitutional Rights.
Frank Barbaro, New York State Assemblyperson, former New York City mayoral candidate.
Elsa Ríos, representative of Madre, member of delegation to Nicaragua, Summer 1984.
Rev. John Mendez, Bapist Pastor, member of delegation to Nicaragua, Summer 1984.
Peter Kornbluh, Research associate, Institute for Policy Studies; author of *Nicaragua: The Price of Intervention*.
Rev. T. Richard Snyder, Professor and Dean, New York Theological Seminary.
Rev. Tomás Tellez, Executive Director of the Nicaraguan Baptist Convention.
Fr. Bob Stark, Catholic priest working with the Central American Historical Institute in Managua.
Richard Garfield, *R.N.*, doctoral candidate in Public Health at Columbia University, worked in Nicaragua with Ministry of Health from April–Dec. 1981 and June–Nov. 1983, co-author of health workers' delegation report on Health and the War in Nicaragua, 1984.
Judy Butler, Staff person on leave from North American Congress on Latin America, currently working with the Nicaraguan Research and Documentation Center for the Atlantic Coast (CIDCA).

TESTIMONY ON BEHALF OF THE U.S. GOVERNMENT

Secretary of State George Shultz or his representative has been invited to present testimony outlining the U.S. government's position with respect to Central America and the Caribbean.

SUMMATION

Including: Neutrality act, 18 USC 959, 960, 962; Ethics in Government Act, 28 USC 591(a); U.S. Constitution, art. I, S8, cl. 11; War Powers Resolution, art. 4(a) et. seq.; Boland Amendment of 1983; Defense Appropriation Act of 1984, S775; U.N. Charter, arts. 1, 2(3), 2(4), 33(1), 51; O.A.S. Charter, arts. 3(b),18,19,20,21; Charter of the International Military Tribunal at Nuremberg, art. 6(a); Inter-American Treaty of Reciprocal Assistance, arts. 1 and 2; Statute of the International Court of Justice, art. 36; Geneva Convention (IV) Relative to the Protection of Civilians; Bilateral Treaty of Friendship, Commerce and Navigation with Nicaragua.

FINDINGS OF FACT TO BE DELIVERED TO THE SECRETARY GENERAL OF THE UNITED NATIONS.

Appendix F:
Excerpts from
Legal Documents

U.S. INSTRUMENTS

The War Powers Clause

U.S. Constitution, Article I, Section 8: The Congress shall have power
. . . [clause 11] to declare war.

United States Neutrality Act,
Conspiracy or Expedition Against a Foreign State

18 USC 956: Conspiracy to injure property of foreign government.

(a) If two or more persons within the jurisdiction of the United States
conspire to injure or destroy specific property situated within a foreign
country and belonging to a foreign government . . . with which the
United States is at peace . . . each of the parties to the conspiracy shall
be fined not more than $5,000 or imprisoned not more than three years,
or both.

18 USC 959: Enlistment in foreign service.

(a) Whoever, within the United States, enlists or enters himself, or hires
or retains another to enlist or enter himself, or to go beyond the jurisdiction of the United States with intent to be enlisted or entered in the
service of any foreign prince, state, colony, district, or people as a
soldier or as a marine or seaman on board any vessel of war, letter of
marque or privateer, shall be fined not more than $1,000 or imprisoned
not more than three years, or both.

18 USC 960: Expedition against friendly nation.

Whoever, within the United States, knowingly begins or sets on foot or
provides or prepares a means for or furnishes the money for, or takes
part in, any military or naval expedition or enterprise to be carried on

from thence against the territory or dominion of any foreign prince or state . . . with whom the United States is at peace, shall be fined not more than $3,000 or imprisoned not more than three years, or both.

United States War Powers Resolution: Reporting Requirements on Hostilities

(50 USC 1541 *et seq.* and 50 USC 1543 [a].)

Section 4 (a): In the absence of a declaration of war, in any case in which United States Armed Forces are introduced —

(1) into hostilities or into a situation where imminent involvement in hostilities is clearly indicated by the circumstances;
(2) into a territory, airspace or waters of a foreign nation, while equipped for combat, except for deployments which relate solely to supply, replacement, repair, or training of such forces: . . .

the President shall submit within 48 hours to the Speaker of the House of Representatives and to the President pro tempore of the Senate a report, in writing . . .

United States Continuing Resolution for Fiscal Year 1983: Boland Amendment, Purpose of Aid to "Contras"

(Public Law 97-377, §793 [1982].)

Section 793: None of the funds provided in this Act may be used by the Central Intelligence Agency or the Department of Defense to furnish military equipment, military training or advice, or other support for military activities, to any group or individual, not part of a country's armed forces, for the purpose of overthrowing the Government of Nicaragua or provoking a military exchange between Nicaragua and Honduras.

United States Foreign Assistance Act: Human Rights Conditions on Security Assistance

(22 USC 2304 [a] [2].)

Section 502B (a) (2): Except under circumstances specified in this section, no security assistance may be provided to any country the government of which engages in a consistent pattern of gross violations of internationally recognized human rights.

(Violations are defined in the section as "torture or cruel, inhuman or degrading treatment or punishment, or prolonged detention without charges or trial, causing the disappearance of persons by the abduction and clandestine detention of those persons, and other flagrant denial of the right to life, liberty or the security of the person.") [22 USC 2304 (d) (1)]

UNITED NATIONS OR WORLD INSTRUMENTS

United Nations Charter

Chapter I: Purposes and Principles
> Article I

The Purposes of the United Nations are:

> 1. To maintain international peace and security, and to that end: to take effective collective measures for the prevention and removal of threats to the peace, and for the suppression of acts of aggression or other breaches of the peace, and to bring about by peaceful means, and in conformity with the principles of justice and international law, adjustment or settlement of international disputes or situations which might lead to a breach of the peace;

> 2. To develop friendly relations among nations based on respect for the principle of equal rights and self-determination of peoples, and to take other appropriate measures to strengthen universal peace;

> 3. To achieve international cooperation in solving international problems of an economic, social, cultural, or humanitarian character, and in promoting and encouraging respect for human rights and for fundamental freedoms for all without distinction as to race, sex, language, or religion. . . .

> Article 2

The Organization and its Members, in pursuit of the Purposes stated in Article 1, shall act in accordance with the following Principles.

> 1. The Organization is based on the principle of the sovereign equality of all its Members.

> 2. All Members, in order to ensure to all of them the rights and benefits resulting from membership, shall fulfill in good faith the obligations assumed by them in accordance with the present Charter.

> 3. All Members shall settle their international disputes by peaceful means in such a manner that international peace and security, and justice, are not endangered.

> 4. All Members shall refrain in their international relations from the threat or use of force against the territorial integrity or political independence of any state, or in any other manner inconsistent with the Purposes of the United Nations.

Chapter VI: Pacific Settlement of Disputes
Article 33
1. The parties to any dispute, the continuance of which is likely to endanger the maintenance of international peace and security, shall, first of all, seek a solution by negotiation, enquiry, mediation, conciliation, arbitration, judicial settlement, resort to regional agencies or arrangements, or other peaceful means of their own choice.

Chapter IX: International Economic and Social Cooperation
Article 55
With a view to the creation of conditions of stability and well-being which are necessary for peaceful and friendly relations among nations based on respect for the principle of equal rights and self-determination of peoples, the United Nations shall promote:
a. higher standards of living, full employment, and conditions of economic and social progress and development;
b. solutions of international economic, social, health, and related problems; and international cultural and educational cooperation; and
c. universal respect for, and observance of, human rights and fundamental freedoms for all without distinction as to race, sex, language, or religion.
Article 56
All members pledge themselves to take joint and separate action in cooperation with the Organization for the achievement of the purposes set forth in Article 55.

Universal Declaration of Human Rights

(Adopted and proclaimed by General Assembly resolution 217 A [III] of 10 December 1948.)

The General Assembly
Proclaims this Universal Declaration of Human Rights as a common standard of achievement for all peoples and all nations, to the end that every individual and every organ of society, keeping this Declaration constantly in mind, shall strive by teaching and education to promote respect for these rights and freedoms and by progressive measures, national and international, to secure their universal and effective recognition and observance, both among the peoples of Member States themselves and among the peoples of territories under their jurisdiction.
Article 2
Everyone is entitled to all the rights and freedoms set forth in this Declaration, without distinction of any kind, such as race, colour, sex,

language, religion, political or other opinion, national or social origin, property, birth or other status.

Furthermore, no distinction shall be made on the basis of the political, jurisdictional or international status of the country or territory to which a person belongs, whether it be independent, trust, non-self-governing or under any other limitation of sovereignty.

Article 3

Everyone has the right to life, liberty and the security of person.

Article 5

No one shall be subjected to torture or to cruel, inhuman or degrading treatment or punishment.

Article 7

All are equal before the law and are entitled without any discrimination to equal protection of the law. All are entitled to equal protection against any discrimination in violation of this Declaration and against any incitement to such discrimination.

Article 8

Everyone has the right to an effective remedy by the competent national tribunals for acts violating the fundamental rights granted him by the constitution or by law.

Article 9

No one shall be subjected to arbitrary arrest, detention or exile.

Article 10

Everyone is entitled in full equality to a fair and public hearing by an independent and impartial tribunal, in the determination of his rights and obligations and of any criminal charge against him.

Article 12

No one shall be subjected to arbitrary interference with his privacy, family, home or correspondence, nor to attacks upon his honour and reputation. Everyone has the right to the protection of the law against such interference or attacks.

Article 13

1. Everyone has the right to freedom of movement and residence within the borders of each State.

2. Everyone has the right to leave any country, including his own, and to return to his country.

Article 14

1. Everyone has the right to seek and to enjoy in other countries asylum from persecution.

2. This right may not be invoked in the case of prosecutions genuinely arising from non-political crimes or from acts contrary to the purposes and principles of the United Nations.

Article 17

1. Everyone has the right to own property alone as well as in association with others.

2. No one shall be arbitrarily deprived of his property.

Article 19

Everyone has the right to freedom of opinion and expression; this right includes freedom to hold opinions without interference and to seek, receive and impart information and ideas through any media and regardless of frontiers.

Article 20

1. Everyone has the right to freedom of peaceful assembly and association.

2. No one may be compelled to belong to an association.

Article 21

1. Everyone has the right to take part in the government of his country, directly or through freely chosen representatives.

2. Everyone has the right of equal access to public service in his country.

3. The will of the people shall be the basis of the authority of government; this will shall be expressed in periodic and genuine elections which shall be by universal and equal suffrage and shall be held by secret vote or by equivalent free voting procedures.

Article 23

1. Everyone has the right to work, to free choice of employment, to just and favourable conditions of work and to protection against unemployment.

Article 25

1. Everyone has the right to a standard of living adequate for the health and well-being of himself and of his family, including food, clothing, housing and medical care and necessary social services, and the right to security in the event of unemployment, sickness, disability, widowhood, old age or other lack of livelihood in circumstances beyond his control.

2. Motherhood and childhood are entitled to special care and assistance. All children, whether born in or out of wedlock, shall enjoy the same social protection.

Article 26

1. Everyone has the right to education. Education shall be free, at least in the elementary and fundamental stages. Elementary education shall be compulsory. Technical and professional education shall be made generally available and higher education shall be equally accessible to all on the basis of merit.

2. Education shall be directed to the full development of the human

personality and to the strengthening of respect for human rights and fundamental freedoms. It shall promote understanding, tolerance and friendship among all nations, racial or religious groups, and shall further the activities of the United Nations for the maintenance of peace.

3. Parents have a prior right to choose the kind of education that shall be given to their children.

Article 27

1. Everyone has the right freely to participate in the cultural life of the community, to enjoy the arts and to share in scientific advancement and its benefits.

2. Everyone has the right to the protection of the moral and material interests resulting from any scientific, literary or artistic production of which he is the author.

Article 30

Nothing in this Declaration may be interpreted as implying for any State, group or person any right to engage in any activity or to perform any act aimed at the destruction of any of the rights and freedoms set forth herein.

International Covenant on Economic, Social and Cultural Rights

(Adopted and opened for signature, ratification and accession by General Assembly resolution 2200 A[XX] of 16 December 1966; entry into force: 3 January 1976.)

Part I
Article 1

1. All peoples have the right of self-determination. By virtue of that right they freely determine their political status and freely pursue their economic, social and cultural development.

Article 4

The States Parties to the present Covenant recognize that, in the enjoyment of those rights provided by the State in conformity with the present Covenant, the State may subject such rights only to such limitations as are determined by law only in so far as this may be compatible with the nature of these rights and solely for the purpose of promoting the general welfare in a democratic society.

Article 5

1. Nothing in the present Covenant may be interpreted as implying for any State, group or person any right to engage in any activity or to perform any act aimed at the destruction of any of the rights or freedoms recognized herein, or at their limitation to a greater extent than is provided for in the present Covenant.

2. No restriction upon or derogation from any of the fundamental human rights recognized or existing in any country in virtue of law, conventions, regulations or custom shall be admitted on the pretext that the present Covenant does not recognize such rights or that it recognizes them to a lesser extent.

Part III
Article 6

1. The States Parties to the present Covenant recognize the right to work, which includes the right of everyone to the opportunity to gain his living by work which he freely chooses or accepts, and will take appropriate steps to safeguard this right.

Article 7

The States Parties to the present Covenant recognize the right of everyone to the enjoyment of just and favorable conditions of work which ensure, in particular:

(a) Remuneration which provides all workers, as a minimum, with:

(i) Fair wages and equal remuneration for work of equal value without distinction of any kind, in particular women being guaranteed conditions of work not inferior to those enjoyed by men, with equal pay for equal work;

(ii) A decent living for themselves and their families in accordance with the provisions of the present Covenant;

(b) Safe and healthy working conditions;

(c) Equal opportunity for everyone to be promoted in his employment to an appropriate higher level, subject to no considerations other than those of seniority and competence;

(d) Rest, leisure and reasonable limitation of working hours and periodic holidays with pay, as well as remuneration for public holidays.

Article 8

1. The States Parties to the present Covenant undertake to ensure:

(a) The right of everyone to form trade unions and join the trade union of his choice, subject only to the rules of the organization concerned, for the promotion and protection of his economic and social interests. No restrictions may be placed on the exercise of this right other than those prescribed by law and which are necessary in a democratic society in the interests of national security or public order or for the protection of the rights and freedoms of others;

(c) The right of trade unions to function freely subject to no limitations other than those prescribed by law and which are necessary in a democratic society in the interests of national security or public order or for the protection of the rights and freedoms of others;

(d) The right to strike, provided that it is exercised in conformity with the laws of the particular country.

2. This article shall not prevent the imposition of lawful restrictions on the exercise of these rights by members of the armed forces or of the police or of the administration of the State.

Article 10

The States Parties to the present Covenant recognize that:

1. The widest possible protection and assistance should be accorded to the family, which is the natural and fundamental group unit of society, particularly for its establishment and while it is responsible for the care and education of dependent children. Marriage must be entered into with the free consent of the intending spouses.

3. Special measures of protection and assistance should be taken on behalf of all children and young persons without any discrimination for reasons of parentage or other conditions. Children and young persons should be protected from economic and social exploitation. Their employment in work harmful to their morals or health or dangerous to life or likely to hamper their normal development should be punishable by law. States should also set age limits below which the paid employment of child labour should be prohibited and punishable by law.

Article 11

1. The States Parties to the present Covenant recognize the right of everyone to an adequate standard of living for himself and his family, including adequate food, clothing and housing, and to the continuous improvement of living conditions. The States Parties will take appropriate steps to ensure the realization of this right, recognizing to this effect the essential importance of international cooperation based on free consent.

2. The States Parties of the present Covenant, recognizing the fundamental right of everyone to be free from hunger, shall take, individually and through international cooperation, the measures, including specific programmes, which are needed:

(a) To improve methods of production, conservation and distribution of food by making full use of technical and scientific knowledge, by disseminating knowledge of the principles of nutrition and by developing or reforming agrarian systems in such a way as to achieve the most efficient developments and utilization of natural resources;

(b) Taking into account the problems of both food-importing and food-exporting countries, to ensure an equitable distribution of world food supplies in relation to need.

Article 12

1. The States Parties to the present Covenant recognize the right of everyone to the enjoyment of the highest attainable standard of physical and mental health.

2. The steps to be taken by the States Parties to the present Covenant to achieve the full realization of this right shall include those necessary for:

(a) The provision for the reduction of the stillbirth-rate and of infant mortality and for the healthy development of the child;

(b) The improvement of all aspects of environmental and industrial hygiene;

(c) The prevention, treatment and control of epidemic, endemic, occupational and other diseases;

(d) The creation of conditions which would assure to all medical service and medical attention in the event of sickness.

Article 13

1. The States Parties to the present Covenant recognize the right of everyone to education. They agree that education shall be directed to the full development of the human personality and the sense of its dignity, and shall strengthen the respect for human rights and fundamental freedoms. They further agree that education shall enable all persons to participate effectively in a free society, promote understanding, tolerance and friendship among all nations and all racial, ethnic or religious groups, and further the activities of the United Nations for the maintenance of peace.

Geneva Convention III: Prisoners of War

(1) Persons taking no active part in the hostilities, including members of armed forces who have laid down their arms and those placed *hors de combat* by sickness, wounds, detention, or any other cause, shall in all circumstances be treated humanely, without any adverse distinction founded on race, colour, religions or faith, sex, birth or wealth, or any other similar criteria.

To this end, the following acts are and shall remain prohibited at any time and in any place whatsoever with respect to the above-mentioned persons:

(a) violence to life and person, in particular murder of all kinds, mutilation, cruel treatment and torture;

(b) taking of hostages;

(c) outrages upon personal dignity, in particular, humiliating and degrading treatment;

(d) the passing of sentences and the carrying out of executions without previous judgment pronounced by a regularly constituted court affording all the judicial guarantees which are recognized as indispensable by civilized peoples.

(2) The wounded and sick shall be collected and cared for.

An impartial humanitarian body, such as the International Committee of the Red Cross, may offer its services to the Parties to the conflict.

The Parties to the conflict should further endeavor to bring into force, by means of special agreements, all or part of the other provisions of the present Convention.

The application of the preceding provisions shall not affect the legal status of the Parties to the conflict.

Article 4

A. Prisoners of war, in the sense of the present Convention, are persons belonging to one of the following categories, who have fallen into the power of the enemy:

(1) Members of the armed forces of a Party to the conflict as well as members of militias or volunteer corps forming part of such armed forces.

(2) Members of other militias and members of other volunteer corps, including those of organized resistance movements, belonging to a Party to the conflict and operating in or outside their own territory, even if this territory is occupied, provided that such militias or volunteer corps, including such organized resistance movements, fulfill the following conditions:

    (a) that of being commanded by a person responsible for his subordinates;

    (b) that of having a fixed distinctive sign recognizable at a distance;

    (c) that of carrying arms openly;

    (d) that of conducting their operations in accordance with the laws and customs of war.

(3) Members of regular armed forces who profess allegiance to a government or an authority not recognized by the Detaining Power.

(4) Persons who accompany the armed forces without actually being members thereof, such as civilian members of military aircraft crews, war correspondents, supply contractors, members of labour units or of services responsible for the welfare of the armed forces, provided that they have received authorization from the armed forces which they accompany, who shall provide them for that purpose with an identity card. . . .

(6) Inhabitants of a non-occupied territory, who on the approach of the enemy spontaneously take up arms to resist the invading forces, without having had time to form themselves into regular armed units, provided they carry arms openly and respect the laws and customs of war.

Geneva Convention IV: Civilians

ARTICLE 30

Protected persons shall have every facility for making application to the Protecting Powers, the International Committee of the Red Cross, the National Red Cross (Red Crescent, Red Lion and Sun) Society of the country where they may be, as well as to any organization that might assist them.

These several organizations shall be granted all facilities for that purpose by the authorities, within the bounds set by military or security considerations.

Apart from the visits of the delegates of the Protecting Powers and of the International Committee of the Red Cross, provided for by Article 143, the Detaining or Occupying Powers shall facilitate as much as possible visits to protected persons by the representatives of other organizations whose object is to give spiritual aid or material relief to such persons.

ARTICLE 31

No physical or moral coercion shall be exercised against protected persons, in particular to obtain information from them or from third parties.

ARTICLE 32

The High Contracting Parties specifically agree that each of them is prohibited from taking any measure of such a character as to cause the physical suffering or extermination of protected persons in their hands. This prohibition applies not only to murder, torture, corporal punishment, mutilation and medical or scientific experiments not necessitated by the medical treatment of a protected person, but also to any other measures of brutality whether applied by civilian or military agents.

ARTICLE 33

No protected person may be punished for an offense he or she has not personally committed. Collective penalties and likewise all measures of intimidation or of terrorism are prohibited.

Pillage is prohibited.

Reprisals against protected persons and their property are prohibited.

ARTICLE 34

The taking of hostages is prohibited.

United Nations General Assembly:
Recent Resolutions on Central America

38/7. The situation in Grenada 11/83
The General Assembly.
1. *Deeply* deplores the armed intervention in Grenada which constitutes a flagrant violation of international law and of the independence, sovereignty, and territorial integrity of that State:
2. *Deplores* the death of innocent civilians resulting from the armed intervention:
3. *Calls upon* all States to show the strictest respect for the sovereignty, independence and territorial integrity of Grenada:

43rd plenary meeting
November 2, 1983

38/10 The situation in Central America: threats to international peace and security and peace initiatives.

The General Assembly.

1. *Reaffirms* the right of all the countries of the region to live in peace and to decide their own future, free from all outside interference or intervention, whatever pretext may be adduced or whatever the circumstances in which they may be committed:

. . .

3. *Condemns* the acts of aggression against the sovereignty, independence and territorial integrity of the States of the region, which have caused losses in human life and irreparable damage to their economies, thereby preventing them from meeting the economic and social development needs of their peoples: especially serious in this context are:

(a) The attacks launched from outside Nicaragua against that country's strategic installations, such as airports and seaports, energy storage facilities and other targets whose destruction seriously affects the country's economic life and endangers densely populated areas:

4. *Urges* the States of the region and other States to desist from or to refrain from initiating military operations intended to exert political pressure which aggravate the situation in the region and hamper the efforts to promote negotiations that the Contadora Group is undertaking with the agreement of the Governments of Central America.

100 plenary meeting
16 December 1983

38/101 Situation of human rights and fundamental freedoms in El Salvador

The General Assembly.

7. *Once again urges* all States to abstain from intervening in the internal situation in El Salvador and to suspend all supplies of arms and any type of military assistance, so as to allow the restoration of peace and security and the establishment of a democratic system based on full respect for human rights and fundamental freedoms:

8. *Expresses its deep concern*: at reports which prove that government forces regularly resort to bombarding urban areas in El Salvador that are not military objectives, and its concern for the fate of several hundred thousand displaced persons who are currently located in camps in which they are subjected to abuse and in which not even the minimum conditions of internment, in terms of either humane treatment or material needs are observed.

100 plenary meeting
16 December, 1983

"Definition of Aggression" Resolution

(United Nations General Assembly resolution 3314.)

Reaffirming the duty of States not to use armed force to deprive peoples of their right to self-determination, freedom and independence, or to disrupt territorial integrity,

Reaffirming also that the territory of a State shall not be violated by being the object, even temporarily, of military occupation or of other measures of force taken by another State in contravention of the Charter, and that it shall not be the object of acquisition by another State resulting from such measures or the threat thereof,

ARTICLE 3: Any of the following acts, regardless of a declaration of war, shall, subject to and in accordance with the provisions of article 2, qualify as an act of aggression:

(a) The invasion or attack by the armed forces of a State of the territory of another State, or any military occupation, however temporary, resulting from such invasion or attack, or any annexation by the use of force of the territory of another State or part thereof;

(b) Bombardment by the armed forces of a State against the territory of another State or the use of any weapons by a State against the territory of another State;

(c) The blockade of the ports or coasts of a State by the armed forces of another State;

(d) An attack by the armed forces of a State on the land, sea or air forces, or marine and air fleets of another State;

(e) The use of armed forces of one State which are within the territory of another State with the agreement of the receiving State, in contravention of the conditions provided for in the agreement or any extension of their presence in such territory beyond the termination of the agreement;

(f) The action of a State in allowing its territory, which it has placed at the disposal of another State, to be used by that other State for perpetrating an act of aggression against a third State;

(g) The sending by or on behalf of a State of armed bands, groups, irregulars or mercenaries, which carry out acts of armed force against another State of such gravity as to amount to the acts listed above, or its substantial involvement therein.

ARTICLE 5:

1. No consideration of whatever nature, whether political, economic, military or otherwise, may serve as a justification for aggression.

2. A war of aggression is a crime against international peace. Aggression gives rise to international responsibility.

3. No territorial acquisition or special advantage resulting from aggression is or shall be recognized as lawful.

Principles of International Law Recognized in the Charter of the Nuremberg Tribunal and in the Judgment of the Tribunal

(Adopted by the International Law Commission of the United Nations, 1950.)

Principle VI

The crimes hereinafter set out are punishable as crimes under international law:

(a) Crimes against peace:

(i) Planning, preparation, initiation or waging of a war of aggression or a war in violation of international treaties, agreements or assurances;

(ii) Participation in a common plan or conspiracy for the accomplishment of any of the acts mentioned under (i).

(b) War crimes:

Violations of the laws or customs of war which include, but are not limited to, murder, ill-treatment or deportation to slave-labour or for any other purpose of civilian population of or in occupied territory, murder or ill-treatment of prisoners of war, of persons on the seas, killing of hostages, plunder of public or private property, wanton destruction of cities, towns or villages, or devastation not justified by military necessity.

(c) Crimes against humanity:

Murder, extermination, enslavement, deportation and other inhuman acts done against any civilian population, or persecutions on political, racial or religious grounds, when such acts are done or such persecutions are carried on in execution of or in connection with any crime against peace or any war crime.

REGIONAL INSTRUMENTS

Charter of the Organization of American States

Chapter IV
Fundamental Rights and Duties of States
ARTICLE 18

No State or group of States has the right to intervene, directly or indirectly, for any reason whatever, in the internal or external affairs of any other State. The foregoing principle prohibits not only armed force but also any other form of interference or attempted threat against the personality of the State or against its political, economic, and cultural elements.

ARTICLE 19

No State may use or encourage the use of coercive measures of an economic or political character in order to force the sovereign will of another State and obtain from it advantages of any kind.

ARTICLE 20

The territory of a State is inviolable; it may not be the object, even temporarily, of military occupation or of other measures of force taken by another State, directly or indirectly, on any grounds whatever. No territorial acquisitions or special advantages obtained either by force or by other means of coercion shall be recognized.

ARTICLE 21

The American States bind themselves in their international relations not to have recourse to the use of force, except in the case of self-defense in accordance with existing treaties or in fulfillment thereof.

American Convention on Human Rights

(Signed November 22, 1969, entered into force July 18, 1978, O.A.S. Treaty Series No. 36 at O.A.S. Off. Rec. OEA/Ser. L./V/II 23 doc. rev. 2.)

ARTICLE 4
Right to Life

1. Every person has the right to have his life respected. This right shall be protected by law and, in general, from the moment of conception. No one shall be arbitrarily deprived of his life.

. . .

6. Every person condemned to death shall have the right to apply for amnesty, pardon, or commutation of sentence, which may be granted in all cases. Capital punishment shall not be imposed while such a petition is pending decision by the competent authority.

ARTICLE 5
Right to Humane Treatment

1. Every person has the right to have his physical, mental, and moral integrity respected.

2. No one shall be subjected to torture or to cruel, inhuman, or degrading punishment or treatment. All persons deprived of their liberty shall be treated with respect for the inherent dignity of the human person.

International Security and Development Cooperation Act of 1981: Certification for Military Aid to El Salvador

(Public Law 97–113, §728; see 22 USC §2370 Notes.)

Section 728(b): In fiscal year 1982 and 1983, funds may be obligated for . . . El Salvador . . . and members of the Armed Forces may be assigned to El Salvador . . . only if the President makes certification in accordance with subsection (d).

   (d) The certification . . . is a determination that the Government of El Salvador—

   (1) is making a concerted, a significant effort to comply with internationally recognized human rights;

   (2) is achieving substantial control over all elements of its armed forces, so as to bring an end . . . to indiscriminate torture and murder . . .

   (3) is making continued progress in . . . land reform . . .

   (4) is committed to the holding of free elections . . .

Appendix G: Organizations Endorsing the War Crimes Tribunal

Brigadista Bulletin
PO Box 450, Prince Street Station
New York, New York 10012

Capuchin Mission Secretariat
1820 Mount Elliot
Detroit, Michigan 48207

Casa El Salvador
PO Box 499, Rockefeller Station
New York, New York 10185

Casa El Salvador Farabundo Martí
PO Box 1769, Madison Square Garden
New York, New York 10159

Christian Peace Conference at the United Nations
777 United Nations Plaza
New York, New York 10017

Committee against Registration and the Draft
National Office
201 Massachusetts Avenue, Northeast
Washington, D.C. 20002

Committee for a Free Chile
PO Box 1121, Cathedral Station
New York, New York 10025

Committee for Chilean Inquiry
415 Grand Street, Apartment E1905
New York, New York 10002

Committee for a Free Grenada
PO Box 1132
New York, New York 10163

Committee in Solidarity with the People of El Salvador
National Office
PO Box 50139
Washington, D.C. 20004

Friends for Jamaica
Box 20392, Cathedral Station
New York, New York 10025

Guardian Newsweekly
33 West 17th Street
New York, New York 10011

Guatemala News and Information Bureau
PO Box 28594
Oakland, California 94604

Indigenous World/El Mundo Indigeno
275 Grandview Avenue
San Francisco, California 94114

Interreligious Fund for Community Organizing
155 Riverside Drive
New York, New York 10027

International Association of Democratic Lawyers
209 West 125th Street
New York, New York 10027

Lawyers Committee Against U.S. Intervention in Central America
863 Massachusetts Avenue, Number 51
Cambridge, Massachusetts 02139

MADRE
853 Broadway
New York, New York 10003

Mobilization for Survival
National Office
853 Broadway, 21st floor
New York, New York 10003

North American Congress on Latin America
151 West 19th Street
New York, New York 10011

National Alliance Against Racist and Political Repression
126 West 119th Street, Suite 101
New York, New York 10026

War Resisters League
National Office
339 Lafayette Street
New York, New York 10012

Womens International League for Peace and Freedom
13 Race Street
Philadelphia, Pennsylvania 19107

LOCAL COMMITTEES AND ORGANIZATIONS

Anti-Repression Resource Team
PO Box 3568
Jackson, Mississippi 39207

Adelante Trading, Inc.
PO Box 1563
New York, New York 10025

Central American Legal Defense Committee
c/o Center for Immigrants' Rights
48 St. Marks Place
New York, New York 10003

Central American Refugee Center of California
123 South Bonnie Brae Street
Los Angeles, California 90057

Central American Refugee Program
115 Diamond Street
San Francisco, California 94114

Center for Immigrants' Rights
48 St. Marks Place
New York, New York 10003

Chelsea Against Nuclear Destruction United
PO Box 332, Old Chelsea Station
New York, New York 10011

Committee for Fair Immigrants' Legislation
Center for Immigrants' Rights
48 St. Marks Place
New York, New York 10003

Committee in Solidarity with the People of El Salvador
Mid-Atlantic Regional Office
19 West 21st Street
New York, New York 10011

David Cortright
National Committee for a Sane Nuclear Policy*
711 G Street, Southeast
Washington, D.C. 20006

National Network in Solidarity with the Nicaraguan People
2025 I Street, Northwest, Suite 402
Washington, D.C. 20006

People's Anti-War Mobilization
19 West 21st Street
New York, New York 10011

Policy Alternatives for the Caribbean and Central America
c/o Institute for Policy Studies
2001 Q Street, Northwest
Washington, D.C. 20009

Puerto Rican Socialist League
PO Box 667, Triborough Station
New York, New York 10035

Revolutionary Socialist League
PO Box 1288, General Post Office
New York, New York 10016

Skylight Pictures
330 West 42nd Street, 24th floor
New York, New York 10036

Social Workers for Peace and Nuclear Disarmament
c/o National Association of Social Workers

---

*Organization listed for identification only

79 Madison Avenue, Room 1707
New York, New York 10016

Union of Democratic Filipinos
4745 43rd Street
Woodside, New York 11377

U.S. Anti-Imperialist League
632 East 23rd Street
Brooklyn, New York 11210

U.S. Out of Central America
2940 16th Street, Suite 7
San Francisco, California 94103

U.S. Peace Council
7 East 15th Street
New York, New York 10003

Committee in Solidarity with the People of El Salvador
New York Office
19 West 21st Street
New York, New York 10011

Committee in Solidarity with the People of El Salvador
4906 Bonnie View
Dallas, Texas 75241

Community Church of New York
40 East 35th Street
New York, New York 10016

Friends of Nicaraguan Culture
PO Box 8305
La Jolla, California 92038

Friends of Nicaraguan Culture
1390 Market Street, Suite 908
San Francisco, California 94102

Friends of the Third World
611 West Wayne Street
Fort Wayne, Indiana 46802

Lexington Task Force on Latin America
PO Box 22003
Lexington, Kentucky 40522

National Association of Social Workers — CA Chapter
204 Avenue B
Redondo Beach, California 90277

New York Circus
2525 Broadway
New York, New York 10025

New York International Work Brigades for Nicaragua
111 Court Street
Brooklyn, New York

North Valley Peacemakers
Box 1133
Oroville, Washington 98844

Orange County Committee on Central America
2019 Crone Avenue
Anaheim, California 92804

PeaceSmith House of Long Island
90 Pennsylvania Avenue
Massapequa, New York 11758

Helen Rodriguez-Trias
800 West End Avenue
New York, New York 10025

About the Editors and Contributors

EDITORS

Paul Ramshaw was one of the organizers of the War Crimes Tribunal on Central America and the Caribbean, was the editor of the *National Lawyers Guild Central America Task Force Newsletter*, and is presently staff attorney at the Federal Appeals Court, San Francisco.

Tom Steers, a journalist, has written for the British and U.S. *Guardian*, *Atlanta Constitution*, Interlink News Service, *Los Angeles Times*, and other periodicals. He is currently a professional staff member of the Newspaper Guild of New York.

Kevin Krajik is a freelance writer and editor based in New York City. His articles on a variety of topics have appeared in *Psychology Today*, *Saturday Review*, *Christian Science Monitor*, and other newspapers and magazines.

CONTRIBUTORS

Robert Armstrong, Executive Director, North American Congress on Latin America.

Father Henry Atkins, Episcopalian Chaplain at Rutgers University.

Leyda Barbieri, associate, Washington Office on Latin America.

Frank Brodhead, co-author of *Demonstration Elections: U.S. Staged Elections in the Dominican Republic, Vietnam and El Salvador*.

Judy Butler, staff member, Nicaraguan Research & Documentation Center for the Atlantic Coast (CIDCA).

Terence Cannon, Center for Legal Education & Urban Policy, City College of New York.

Charles Clements, M.D., Vietnam Veteran, Faculty Member at Albert Einstein College of Medicine and at the Department of Social Medicine at Montefiore Medical Center, practiced medicine in FMLN-controlled territory in El Salvador in 1982–83.

Ramón Flores, Salvadoran medical student, former prisoner, and torture victim.

Jane Franklin, Co-editor, *Cuba Update*.

Richard Garfield, R. N., School of Epidemiology, Columbia University.

Peter Kornbluh, research associate, Institute for Policy Studies.

Frank LaRue, exiled Guatemalan labor lawyer.

David MacMichael, former CIA analyst on Central America.

Joachim Mark, Grenadian historian.

Harold Mayerson, attorney.

Rigoberta Menchú, Guatemalan Indian leader from El Quiché Province.

Raúl Molina, exiled professor of Engineering, dean and rector at the University of San Carlos, Guatemala.

Tommie Sue Montgomery, professor of political science, Dickinson College.

Salvador Orochena, Nicaraguan student leader exiled by Somoza in 1971.

Joanne Palmisano, M.D., professor, Downstate Medical Center, State University of New York.

Héctor Recinos, Salvadoran refugee, son of imprisoned labor leader.

Hazel Ross, Legislative Liaison for Economic Affairs, TransAfrica.

Margarita Samad-Matías, Director of Latin America & Caribbean Studies Program, City College of New York.

William Schaap, co-editor, *Covert Action*.

Father Bob Stark, staff member, Central American Historical Institute, Managua, Nicaragua.

Reverend Tomás Tellez, Executive Director, Nicaraguan Baptist Convention.

Richard Alan White, senior fellow Council on Hemispheric Affairs.